Peop

For anyone looking for a comprehensive guide to Digital Marketing Tactics, this is it. **–Lauren Sudworth, Senior Content Strategy Manager, Hootsuite**

As you will see from the takeaways inside these pages, the advice provided is well grounded, well-tested and effective. Whether it is amplifying news with news release distribution, creating influencer programs or understanding the latest SEO and social opportunities, the tips from Media Leaders' conferences are one of the first places we look to see what is and is not working. **–Serena Ehrlich, Director of Social and Evolving Media, Business Wire**

This book is full of tips digital marketers can use to be more authentic when communicating with their customers. **–Kyle Snarr, Director of Brand Communication, Flipboard**

This book offers actionable tips that you can use immediately to gain results whether you're a small business or large enterprise. **–Amisha Gandhi, Senior Director, Influencer Marketing, SAP**

This is the book everyone should read to learn the insider tricks for using social media to your advantage. Great collection of ideas and insights! **–Jock Breitwieser, Head of Corporate Communications, TriNet**

Digital Marketing Tactics

600 digital tactics from 150+ speakers at our marketing conferences in California

Version 1.0
by Josh Ochs &
The MediaLeaders.com Team

Copyright Media Leaders, LLC 2017
Distribution of this book without written permission is strictly prohibited.

WATCH THE VIDEO SESSIONS FROM THIS BOOK FREE!

READ THIS FIRST

Just to say thanks for buying this book, we would like to give you the video sessions from our conferences 100% FREE!

TO DOWNLOAD GO TO:

MediaLeaders.com/dmt/videos/

Fellow Marketer,

I set a goal in 2012 to become the best marketer I could become.

To do this, I knew I needed to surround myself with great marketers.

Josh Ochs
Founder,
MediaLeaders.com

My friends and I started hosting conferences to ask people we admired to share their techniques.

Essentially, we made a lineup we would love to listen to (and be able to sit in the front row and take notes).

My friends and I designed our conferences to be tactical, and full of helpful techniques professionals can immediately put to use in their business.

Thanks to the help of our presenters, we now are able to feature over 150 thought leaders each year who share their expertise at our events in California.

Our experts bring their best tactical knowledge in the digital marketing space and generously share their techniques with our attendees.

We then record each session and share it online for people to learn all over the country via YouTube and our blog.

But blog posts aren't enough.

We then spend dozens of hours summarizing all the panel discussions, sessions (and our favorite blog posts) and put them together into this book for you to enjoy offline.

There's 600+ tactical tips in this book and they are organized into three parts.

Three parts of this book:
Engage, Influence and Analyze.

It is my hope that this book gives you a few tips to become a better digital marketer and also teach you how to use digital tools to scale your marketing message (to reach more prospects).

I hope you enjoy this book as much as I have.

See you at our next conference.

Sincerely,
-Josh Ochs and the Team at MediaLeaders.com

P.S. Our digital safety website is a big hit with parents and educators. Many of the digital marketing tactics we learned in this book helped us to grow our safety message's reach to 500,000 parents each year. If you know a parent of a teen, please send them to our website at SafeSmartSocial.com to help them keep their kids safe.

P.P.S. Access all of the videos from this book for FREE by visiting: MediaLeaders.com/dmt/videos/

Table of Contents

Want to be featured in the next version of this book?

Become a thought leader at one of our next events to be included in our next Digital Marketing Tactics book. We release this book twice a year (and it is read by professionals all over the world).

Visit MediaLeaders.com/Sponsor to learn more

Here's what you get at the event:
- Present on a panel discussion alongside 3+ experts in our main room (share your tactical tips on our main stage with other pros).
- Lead a breakout session/class (the stage is all yours) on a topic using slides in front of a dedicated 30 minute class. Media Leaders will record this class and post it online.

Post event thought leadership:
- Get additional tickets to the conference to invite clients/prospects to listen and learn from you.
- Video footage/file of the class sent to you after the event to download and use as you see fit.
- Highlight reel/edited version of the video footage on MediaLeaders.com
- Actionable key takeaways of the presentation posted on MediaLeaders.com.

Part 1: Engage

When it comes to marketing in the digital realm, it's all about engagement–engaging with reporters, consumers, and influencers or just regular people on social media who get excited about your brand and want to share it. We designed these panels for you to learn from the experts who will share their best advice for achieving these goals and more.

2017 Trends You Need to Know in PR, Search & Social

Presented by:
Serena Ehrlich, Director, Social and Evolving Media, Business Wire

Here are some key takeaways from this topic:

- **News surpasses social media** as the #1 thing people do on mobile.
- **Engage consumers by speaking their language**
  If you want to engage consumers, you must speak their language and their language is becoming increasingly visual.
- **Google puts the news at the top of search**
  Google loves news and news releases and prioritizes them to the top of your search results.
- **Amplify your content on LinkedIn**
  Create LinkedIn "breaking news" and ask friends to share the same piece of content, within a five-minute span, as you.
- **Always add an image to your Twitter posts**
  Use images to explain visually what the text in your tweet is trying to communicate.
- **Don't be afraid of social sharing**
  Continuously share content on social. Since social media is in real-time, posting your content once on Twitter doesn't necessarily mean all your followers saw that tweet.

- **Segment your audience on Facebook**
  Create personalized Facebook updates for your different demographics.
- **If you sell to small businesses, utilize SlideShare**
  Posting best practices and tutorials on SlideShare is a great way to target small businesses.
- **Pinterest has an extremely high CTR**
  Always include links to your site behind your images so you can funnel traffic from Pinterest back to your site.
- **Only use Snapchat if your audience is 18-34 years old**
  If your audience is 18-34 then use Snapchat to provide exclusives, promote events, and show demos.
- **Create videos showcasing your product**
  Mix pre-created footage with live footage for a more authentic feel.

2017 is the year of news content visibility. When you distribute news, you get analytics and that tells you who opens news, who cares about news, and you can take that information and use it.

PR generates exceptional impact. Most people are used to working at companies that have a big marketing budget and a tiny PR budget. That has got to change. PR people need bigger budgets and the reason for that is that the #1 thing that travels today is news. In fact, a new study came out that said that the number one thing that people do on mobile phones is news consumption (which beat out social media, the previous #1). News on its own has a 63% trust rating, but when it is shared via social media or email between friends, it has an 83% trust rating.

Consumers have changed. If you are under the age of 36, you are the first generation that had computers in your house. Today's consumers are experts in Google search. Before phones, the sales process was a 7-touch sales process. It is now a 22-touch sales process. Someone must see your company, your brand 22 times before they will make a purchase. Today's consumers because of this expertise, they do their own research, they rely on their own research results, and they trust consumers (their recommendations from friends). This is where search and social become important because they make it easy for people to share their thoughts and opinions.

These devices have made us visually fluent. Public relations is typically text-based communications. That must change. Visual learners make up 63% of the world, which means that they learn through visual interaction. Every time you put out a text-only status update or news update, what have you done? You have excluded 63% of the world. If you want to engage consumers, you must speak their language and their language is becoming increasingly visual. Emoji's and Snapchat are working so well because they require no knowledge of any language. It's a visual communication platform. We need to start speaking in both text and visual as PR people.

Google loves editorial coverage. Google loves press releases, and so every time that you get editorial coverage, not only should you count that as a "win," but you need to tell your leaders or management that that coverage had SEO. That coverage was at the top of search. News releases do not have traditional SEO, but they have search ability. Google recognized what users are looking for in search and when a user searches for a company or business name, they know that users want to find the business website, a couple of key pages within the site, the social channels, and the news. Google puts the news and any coverage that you secure at the top of a search.

We all know that social is a terrific way to distribute and get information amplified, but there are tricks for every single platform for getting your information shared. I'll start with LinkedIn. LinkedIn has two free ways to get your information out. First, LinkedIn user's aspirational goals for the channel are competitive. They pay attention to what others are doing. If you are the editorial contact on a news release or the quoted source on a news release or an article, LinkedIn is scraping the web for these pieces and showing them to you. How many of you guys have ever gotten an email from LinkedIn saying "You are in the news." This is LinkedIn telling you "Congratulations!" but they also send this information to all your contacts. It's a great way to optimize the network, but here's the thing: a lot of our clients will submit a news release and they will quote the CEO and the CEO has no LinkedIn presence. Consider adding a second quote from perhaps your head of sales or someone else who has a robust LinkedIn profile. Leverage that. (Note: This does not work if you use a middle initial with your name so take those out).

Another LinkedIn trick. Find five or six friends and connect offline. Ask them to share the same piece of news that you do around the same time. LinkedIn thinks it is "breaking news" when they see people connected on LinkedIn sharing the same news in a five-minute span. Then it puts these "news" items on the wall of your contacts when they login. It doesn't have to be a press release or news release, either. It can be any form of content, even a hiring page.

The aspiration on Twitter is to be the first, the smartest, or the funniest. The tweets that get the retweets, are the ones that surprise you, shock you, or the ones that have data so good for your industry that you must be the one that shares it. Twitter now allows you to add multimedia, start a tweet with an @ sign, and none of that impacts the visibility or takes up the character count online.

Always add an image on Twitter. Create a tweet that is a mix of visuals and text. Use the image to explain visually what the text we have up there is. GIF files also work extremely well. Add ironic GIF files and people love it. Stats also do very, very well on Twitter.

Need coverage? Op-Eds. If you can't get people to cover your story, op-eds. I've placed 600 op-eds in five years. Every piece of coverage I get, I share a minimum of 15 times on social. Social is real-time and if someone isn't looking at that moment, they won't see Tweet #1, they might see Tweet #5. I have no shame in my sharing game. Shame in the sharing game is the downside of a lot of companies.

Facebook: Personal, Smart, Visual. Know that women, men, young people, and old people will buy your product for different reasons. Write a status update for each market. Facebook allows you to do status updates by demographic. Target your audience.

Facebook Pay-for-Play. Keep in mind that the words in your update matter. If you can put the top words of the day in your update, it will be more likely to show up at the top of Facebook's newsfeed and at the top of the Home page for your customers. Content type also impacts your visibility. You need to test your type and determine what your audience pays attention to the most.

The best performing Facebook Live broadcasts average over ten minutes in length and include surprise materials at key points starting at 90 seconds. 100% of your fans get the notice that you are "Live" and they see the notification that you write out about why you are going Live so make sure that it's really good and interesting. They will alert your whole fan page.

Instagram's aspiration is fame. The metric for success is how many "likes" you get. The reality is that because of likes and the aspect of fame, consider creating a program that rewards your employees or your customers for posting. Sharing photos is huge and builds loyalty and advocates out of users.

SlideShare is where people go to learn. It might seem old-fashioned, but if you sell to a small business, then you want to share here. Small businesses want to be smarter and so a SlideShare with best practices or "How To's" do really well here.

Pinterest is for showing and showing-off. It tells the world "who we are." Clients always tell me, "Well, we don't use Pinterest because they don't show up on our analytics." Do you know why? Because people do not put URLs behind their photos so when users click on the photos, a bigger photo pops up rather than taking them to the website. Your analytics will change if you do this. Pinterest has an extremely high CTR and it is ignored routinely by big companies.

Snapchat is the unvarnished truth. 71% of users are ages 18-34. Snapchat is where you want to provide VIP/exclusive access, promote events, show cool demos, be highly relevant, and include offers and coupons. Don't spend time here if your audience is not in this age range.

Reddit's users aspire to be passionate, smart, and informed. Reddit is not a network where you simply throw out information. You must listen. Reddit is a large audience with 45,000 targeted communities. Be authentic.

YouTube + BizWireTV offer video news for consumers. Create content for all parts of your sales funnel. Determine what your audience watches in long form and then shorten it. Make accessible videos by showing the usage of your product, but also in a short amount of time. Shrink it down.

There are some great bonus free tools that you can use to help with trends in PR, search, and social:

Headline Testers
Aminstitute.com/headline
CoSchedule.com/headline-analyzer

How far did my URL travel?
LinkTally.com
TweetResearch.com

Multimedia Testers
Popularity.csail.mit.edu

Keyword Identification
GoodKeywords.com/trends
Google.com/trends
Google.com/trends/HotTrends
TrendsMap.com
Youtube.com/TrendsDashboard
Trendy24.in

Growing Your Social Following

Here are some key takeaways from this topic:

- **Focus on providing relevant content**
  The number of social media followers and likes an account has is becoming less prevalent; instead, audiences are focusing on finding valuable and relevant content. Create content with the goal of engaging and building a relationship with your followers.
- **Determine what your audience likes**
  Social media can be a great tool for determining what content your audience likes. Once you've found what content your audience most engages with then you can start to create content tailored to your audience preferences.
- **Don't release content just for the sake of releasing content**
  Have a strategy in place before you start to distribute content on social. Create each social media post with a specific goal in mind so you avoid creating irrelevant content.

Watch these videos on our website: Get these session videos delivered to your inbox by registering this book at MediaLeaders.com/dmt/videos/ (and be the first to hear about our next events).

Q: What is important now in social media? What is working in social and what isn't? Should the end game be growing followers and likes, or is there something more?

Social is still alive and well, but it has changed. While the focus used to be on the number of likes and followers you had, it's less about that now and more about creating really great content. Ultimately, the goal is to build a relationship with your customers, your clients, your followers, and your users. I see a lot of brands that try to shout out their own message and talk about themselves, but really try to listen to your followers and build a relationship with them by providing content that fills an unmet need. **–Cynthia Rojas, Hype Digital Marketing**

Specifically, in entertainment, we tell stories about other stories. A social following is now what we refer to as a vanity metric so we don't really try to build a social following, we just really have to mine and figure out where these stories are and where we can seek them out to build that connection with an audience. **–Nick Mazzucco, Ignition Creative**

The thing that I am most excited about right now is influencer marketing and brand ambassadorship. There is so much potential there. I do think that followers and likes still matter and you should be trying to get those counts up because it's a key part of "social proof" and so if you want to keep people engaging with your brand, you need to keep those numbers high. **–Kristi Kellogg, Bruce Clay, Inc.**

Q: What is an example of using social media to market projects?

We were fortunate to work on a major superhero show in the past year for Netflix where we had to figure out why people would go from Season 1 to Season 2 and what was it that they really liked about the show? We found out that they really responded to the more realistic and grittier aspects of the show as well as the idea that the main character was a conflicted Catholic. It became this test of when does right become wrong? We used that to develop our narrative base throughout the entire campaign. We listened on social to develop that better narrative marketing by using tools such as Netbase. **–Nick Mazzucco, Ignition Creative**

Q: What are some tools that you can use to grow your social following and encourage social media engagement?

Some specific tools for Twitter are Tweepi.com and Manageflitter.com. Both of those tools do the same types of things including letting you see who is following you, sort your followers by influence, sort by industry, track the followers of followers, do competitive analysis, and more. On Instagram, I am loving a tool called Instagress.com. There is another called Iconosquare.com as well, but it's a bit pricier. These tools let you look at who is following you, how they are following you, and more. **–Kristi Kellogg, Bruce Clay, Inc.**

One of the tools that we use a lot is Buzzsumo.com. It's great for a number of things, including using it to see what content trends are rising to the top in your particular category. This is very helpful when trying to build an effective content strategy. I also love using it to build influencer marketing strategies by putting in what category I need to build a list around. It will put together a list of the top influencers in that category with trends, analytics, and more. **–Cynthia Rojas, Hype Digital Marketing**

Q: What is something that you should not do on social?

You have to test everything. One of the things that Instagress does is it lets you take your profile and write whatever kind of comment that you want and then target people or hashtags or locations. You can turn it on to be automatic. In my case, I did this with my personal Instagram and I was too lenient with the hashtags. I wanted to interact with too many and people put hashtags on things that I would never have normally liked or interacted with. It was a disaster. So, you need to be more stringent when you use automatic tools. **–Kristi Kellogg Bruce Clay, Inc.**

I think the times that this topic has gone wrong for us as a company, regardless of the client, are the times where we do not clearly map out a brand strategy before we are doing the content push and it becomes pushing out content just for the sake of content. We have found that the most successful campaigns are really deconstructed content-wise and more organic. You don't want it to look like an ad. We want photos that look like they are taken in real time. **– Cynthia Rojas, Hype Digital Marketing**

Q: How do you plan your social? How do you schedule?

There is a tool called <u>CoSchedule.com</u> that's a plugin for WordPress and allows you to post to everything (except Instagram) right there in WordPress. With CoSchedule you can see your content really nicely on a calendar, so I like that a lot. We like to plan out posts on a spreadsheet for our clients and then we schedule them for the month. **–Kristi Kellogg, Bruce Clay, Inc.**

We start as a brainstorm and then our social media managers and community managers use the spreadsheet to mark out the calendar on what they are going to do. Then we come back in and start analyzing the data after the fact. Based on our analysis, we make changes. **–Nick Mazzucco, Ignition Creative**

Do you know how your customers see your brand online?

Our team works with brands of all sizes to ensure their brand message is Light, Bright and Polite®.

Get a digital brand audit from our team to see how your customers are finding you (and what they think about your online footprint).

Visit MediaLeaders.com/Audit

Our online audit includes:

10 page customized report with your brand's online footprint

- We show you positive mentions that can be utilized for content marketing
- We highlight negative results and give you multiple suggestions on how to remove them
- We provide a custom video library designed to help your brand to improve its online footprint
- Also learn:
  - How content marketing can build a pipeline of prospects
  - Influencer marketing tips
  - Social media tips for reputation management
  - 5 key tips your brand can use to improve your online presence

Visit MediaLeaders.com/Audit to learn more

Branding on Instagram & Snapchat

Here are some key takeaways from this topic:

- **Choose your platform wisely**
  Instagram is the place to put your beautifully curated content because on Instagram your content will live forever. Snapchat, however, can create a sense of immediacy–which is great for building in a call to action. So, build content for the platform you want to use.
- **Be authentic**
  Show behind-the-scenes stories, real people from your company, etc. Viewers are turned off by pushy, salesy tactics.
- **Build influencer relationships**
  If you find influencers whose lifestyle aligns with your brand and build relationships with them, they're your best bet for reaching your target audience in an organic way.
- **Tell a story**
  Snapchat posts come and go quickly, but you don't have to present your message all at once. Instead create a beginning, middle, and end, and spread out in a sequence.
- **Be creative in finding KPIs**
  On Snapchat, for instance, traditional indicators aren't really available, so you should find ways to watch audience behavior around your marketing efforts.

Q: How do you use Instagram and Snapchat? Do you think one is better suited for a particular strategy than the other?

I think with Instagram we are seeing that it is a lot more posed. People want a picture-perfect image of their life out there on Instagram, whereas Snapchat is a little bit more authentic, real-time, and unapologetic. I think that is how brands and influencers are seeing it too. Snapchat is more for engaging people in the moment, while Instagram is putting your best self forward and seeing how people respond. **–Rachael Cihlar, TapInfluence**

When I look at the two platforms, they are both really in their infancy as an advertising program. Instagram rolled out ads in September of last year, but the value of theirs is that you have the full toolset that you have on Facebook. You can do lookalike, customizes, and it is easy to track. Snapchat is new, all ads are skippable and attribution is fairly poor, but people are consuming content in a way that is more natural and engagement is incredibly high. **–Ryan Faber, Growth Marketer, Entrepreneur & Investor**

Q: What are some favorite tips and trends for brands who want to use Snapchat for marketing?

Only 6% of brands are actually utilizing Snapchat for this business right now, so there is a huge opportunity, but it only makes sense if your audience is there. Snapchat is mostly millennials, really young people, teens, and high schoolers. **–Kristi Kellogg, Bruce Clay, Inc.**

With any social media channel, as it continues to emerge it will grow into different demographics. So, while Snapchat does skew young, we are seeing that the highest growth is in the 30+ category. If you get in early, there might be opportunities down the line as it continues to expand. Among brands that I see doing the best content in Snapchat, the key is that they are creating stories–they present a full story with a beginning, middle, and end as well as a daily theme. That sets them apart. **–Sae Cho, Horizon Media**

To develop content and utilize it effectively on Snapchat, post things organically. For example, backstage at New York Fashion Week is something we always do so we can post behind-the-scenes interviews, photos, and things like that. But if you are a brand with multiple locations, it would be worth it for you to look at an overarching Snapchat strategy that would allow different people from your different locations to participate. That way you have more well-rounded content. **–Breanna Collier, TONI&GUY**

Q: What are the best practices for using Instagram?

I think you have an overarching story, a platform like Instagram is a great way to be able to use sub-stories of your longer-form content to get the word out there and then point over to the longer-form content. Instagram also has a generally higher engagement level than some of the other video platforms. I would recommend video always as a part of your strategy for Instagram. **–Sean Williams, BuzzFeed**

The most important thing for Instagram is to act like an organic user. Successful posts are those that are shot with a unique point of view, tell a story, use filters and that are a square as opposed to the other dimensions that people use, because that is what people expect to see. Don't be salesy, because then you are no longer part of the native Instagram experience, and you will be ignored. We know that 60% of people have learned about a product or service through Instagram and 75% of people actually go take the next step and search for your business, go to your website, or make a purchase. **–Kristi Kellogg, Bruce Clay, Inc.**

Instagram is the place to put your beautifully curated content, because on Instagram, your content will live forever whereas on Snapchat it lives for 24 hours. You want to have well edited, concise photos and a caption with a strategy. As advertising becomes more prevalent on Instagram, businesses are jumping in without first creating ads that are less sales-pitch oriented and more contest-oriented or other more organic methods. 60-second videos are also great for sharing tutorials, behind-the-scenes footage, and look books. **–Breanna Collier, TONI&GUY**

Instagram is about creating an entire lifestyle. If your product is a pristine, clean cocktail beverage, you need to think about where you are having that cocktail–is it on a patio? At the beach? With a book, next to it? Engagement rate actually tends to be higher when the product is smaller in the photo because it feels more authentic to Instagram users, so keep in mind the importance of the lifestyle component. Take the time as well to engage by commenting back to any comments that you receive and really listen to what users are saying about your brand. **–Sae Cho, Horizon Media**

Q: Are there other tips you've seen work well for brands posting their own content or working with influencers on either Instagram or Snapchat?

Authenticity is key. The more authentic stories and authentic photos work best. **–Sean Williams, BuzzFeed**

As a business, we get the most engagement when we show pictures of people who work at our company. So, you must think creatively about how to make authentic and organic content. Then from a personal standpoint, I started doing way more hashtag research and using hashtags strategically as a person, and I have gotten so much more engagement. **–Kristi Kellogg, Bruce Clay, Inc.**

Calls to Action. The best thing about Snapchat is that it is only around for 24 hours, so there is already a built-in sense of urgency with your content. If you can build in those calls to action, you will see better results because people are already incentivized to act quickly on Snapchat. **–Sae Cho, Horizon Media**

How should brands reach out to influencers? Any best practices there?

With Snapchat, an influencer endorsement is usually more influential and cost effective when compared to ads, which can cost as much as $750K to start with for a single day of marketing. But targeting with influencers can be tough. I think the best thing is to look for an influencer whose lifestyle aligns with your brand, look at their creative aesthetic, their captions, and the language that they use to respond to their fans. A "takeover" is a great way to bring the influencer's followers over to your channel. The influencer typically starts by posting a small story on their account first to say, "Hey I'm going to be taking over the Jack and the Box's Snapchat handle today to give you a behind-the-scenes look," and then they will publish that and migrate their audience over to the brand's Snapchat handle. **–Sae Cho, Horizon Media**

Make sure that you let the influencer do what they do best and do not assert too much control over them. What we have found is if you are too heavy-handed with an influencer, their audience is going to shy away from your brand rather than be attracted to it. **–Sean Williams, BuzzFeed**

If you are a smaller brand or your budget isn't as large, there is something I like to use called PeopleMap. You can go through and look at your competitors' lists and people in your target market. You can start targeting influencers with fewer followers–less than 20,000 for example–and reach out to them by individually offering them a service, product or fun event opportunity. **–Breanna Collier, TONI&GUY**

If you are trying to connect with an influencer, first try to create a meaningful relationship with them. That doesn't start by asking them to do something for you. Give value to them by sharing and retweeting their content. **–Kristi Kellogg, Bruce Clay, Inc.**

Building a relationship is important. Interviev
an article is a great way. **–Jesse Leimgruber,**

**Q: Let's talk about some of the metrics: freq
posting, time of day, etc. What are your opir
best practices that brands should follow to run their own
brand's account?**

Personally, I think it will differ by account and brand, so the
best thing that you can do for yourself is really measure and
take the time to analyze. Test your engagement. **–Sae Cho,
Horizon Media**

Do a lot of experimenting. **–Sean Williams, BuzzFeed**

The good thing about Snapchat is that you can post as
much content as you are comfortable with because the user
has to go in and grab it from you. With Instagram, I use the
Simply Measured free Instagram report. As far as scheduling,
I love using Planoly, which allows you to schedule content
and move it around to see which photos are going to look
best next to one another in the feed. We also like UNUM for
Instagram feed planning. **–Breanna Collier, TONI&GUY**

Change out the link that is in your profile often. **–Sean
Williams, BuzzFeed**

Make sure you are social listening, and you can use memes
and reframe them to fit your brand to help with cultural
relevance. **–Sae Cho, Horizon Media**

...of successful campaigns I have seen require that the ...er screenshot or tweet something specific to ramp up engagement. **–Jesse Leimgruber, NeoReach**

Q: How are social platforms changing?

I think the biggest shift has been from static images to videos, which really helps with the storytelling process and creating a narrative around your brand. The older demographic is growing daily on Snapchat and I think the content is also starting to mature as well. **–Sean Williams, BuzzFeed**

Social is becoming more about a one-on-one relationship with brands, and this needs to change the way that brands market themselves to consumers. Make sure you engage with your users as soon as they respond to you. **–Breanna Collier, TONI&GUY**

Q: What are the top metrics you are looking at to make sure that you are successful?

Conversions and traffic to your site. **–Kristi Kellogg, Bruce Clay, Inc.**

Those are the most valuable. **–Jesse Leimgruber, NeoReach**

Q: Do you have any use cases or experiences where you think "I'm glad I tried this, but boy was I off"?

Your content is really important. Sometimes you post a piece where you think you are showcasing the product and you are not. I had a product, which was an audio Bluetooth speaker that looked like a silver pillar, and the idea was that it was supposed to be kind of hidden in your living room or kitchen. But then how do you showcase that? We had to do a lot of testing to figure out what worked and what didn't. We had to take it out of its natural environment. Since it is portable, we took it to the beach. That worked in the Instagram space in a way that showing the product in its natural environment, your home or your kitchen, didn't. – **Jennifer Winberg, Marketing Consultant**

Don't force it. You don't always need an app, you don't always need to be on Snapchat. Evaluate these platforms and see how it could work, but don't force it. The most important thing to think about is the medium. What happens a lot is I think someone has an ad campaign and they just bolt it onto the platform and it doesn't make sense. Build content specific for the platform you are going to use. When we make something, we film something specifically for TV, specifically for Snapchat, and specifically for Instagram. **–Ryan Faber, Growth Marketer, Entrepreneur & Investor**

Q: How do I measure my success? What kind of KPIs can I share and what are the metrics that I can use?

Instagram has full attribution. You can see what people are clicking on and understand exactly what is happening. Snapchat, on the other hand, is very difficult. You get "wow" numbers. You don't know how many people are being driven to your site, your product, or your service. It is very hard to measure what impact you have had. One way that you can try to track it is by trying to see unique identifiers on mobile devices where you can try to match it up to new users. It's a rough match, but they are working on it. **–Ryan Faber, Growth Marketer, Entrepreneur & Investor**

Snapchat does become harder because they don't share as much information. If you have a CMO who really wants that data and you can't get it, one thing that you can do is show anecdotal evidence of engagement. I worked on a campaign for Wolverine when Snapchat was very new and ended up taking screen captures of all of these times when fans were Snapchatting these Wolverine hands they had drawn, and I put that together. I said, "We don't have the analytics yet, but I can show you the degree to which these fans are interacting with this." We had fans responding, taking a picture, drawing Wolverine hands, and then snapping it back to us. It was easy to see that there was an extreme level of engagement. **–Jennifer Winberg, Marketing Consultant**

Q: When you think about the campaigns that you can potentially build, what would you recommend for someone in the B2B space for an easy way to construct a campaign and dip their toes in without risking too much?

Most of you probably collect email addresses from people. Use that as a custom audience list. Build that into Facebook. You can target those people exactly with whatever message you want. Most likely they will be on Instagram or Facebook. You can load it in that custom audience list of people. The second one is if you have a list of emails of high-value customers, you can use a lookalike audience. Finally, try XIntent. XIntent looks at mouse patterns and tries to predict when someone is going to leave the page. Then it provides an offer and captures that email address. **–Ryan Faber, Growth Marketer, Entrepreneur & Investor**

Snapchat Stories vs. Instagram Stories

Here are some key takeaways from this topic:

- **Focus on the platform that your audience engages with most**
  Your brand doesn't necessarily need to be on both Instagram and Snapchat. Pay attention to which platform your audience engages with most and focus on creating valuable content for that platform.
- **Incorporate your posts across platforms**
  Some of the most successful and engaging campaigns have encouraged their audience to participate across multiple platforms, not just on Snapchat or Instagram.
- **Share newsworthy content on Snapchat**
  Newsworthy content is popular on Snapchat but if you don't have news to share, find creative ways to get your brand out there. Consider creating a Snapchat geofilter to encourage audience engagement.

Watch these videos on our website: Get these session videos delivered to your inbox by registering this book at MediaLeaders.com/dmt/videos/ (and be the first to hear about our next events).

Q: Instagram or Snapchat? What is the difference and why choose one over the other?

Numbers do not lie. If you look at a company like Facebook who owns Instagram, and has 1.8 billion active users worldwide then you can see that it is a powerful tool. Instagram is riding the coattails of that success and they have direct integration into the platform. That said, Snapchat is doing really exciting work engaging much younger demographics in a really effective way with a highly-engaged platform. As a content creator who is focused heavily on distribution of content and branded content solutions, both are viable and worth using. **–Josh Baird, Director, FOX Sports**

I would say it really depends on where your audience is. If they are more on Instagram stories, be there. If they are more on Snapchat stories, be there. Each platform has its own pros and cons. Snapchat has better facial recognition and complex filters that you can use, but then Instagram has a more intuitive UI. Also, Instagram stories are in their infancy having just come out in August of 2016 so I don't think we can have a definitive answer for who is going to succeed at this point. **–Kristi Kellogg, Clay, Inc.**

Q: How do you market yourself through Snapchat stories and Instagram stories? What are some strategies that you can use with Snapchat and Instagram?

There are great, real, newsy stories on Snapchat, which is awesome. Thirty percent of Snapchat users followed the 2016 election on Snapchat and the stories around each event along the way, but what do you do if you are not producing content that is newsworthy? Soul Cycle purchased geo-filters and so all of the people working out at a single location can take a snap after their workout and use the "SoulCycle Summer of Soul" filter before sharing that snap. It's a different way to get your brand out there on Snapchat without sharing a story. A tool that can help create Snapchat geofilters is called PepperFilters.com and they have templates that you can use to create filters. Canva.com also helps you create your own filters. **–Kristi Kellogg, Bruce Clay, Inc.**

In my mind, the best application for Snapchat to date from a brand level, is what I have seen Call of Duty do. They went back into one of their previous titles and dropped in an update that had a Snapcode. Now, the PR team and the social media team seeded out hints that there was something waiting for players if they could find it in this game. Now gamers were going through, replaying the level, talking about it, and it's everywhere - forums, social media, private messages amongst gamers. Once they discover the code, they take a picture of it and it's the trailer for the upcoming game. So, Snapchat was the catalyst, but it wasn't the entirety of the campaign. It was probably the primary touchpoint, but it was a PR and social media campaign as well. I think Snapchat can only be a part of ROI if it fits into a larger ecosystem. **–Justin Celko, Blitz**

I really believe that you get what you measure. Try to make social media decisions for the team based on data. Decide how you can allocate resources across platforms and be realistic. For us, Snapchat is there and we want to be a part of it, but we recognize that it is part of a larger social media world. It's a matter of figuring out where your audience is, making that decision, and then going in. **–Josh Baird, FOX Sports**

As a content creator, I want both platforms to flourish. Instagram and Snapchat gives designers, videographers, motion graphic animators and other creatives a wider toolkit to tap into. You can come up with new ways to tell stories by coming up with Easter egg ideas, filters, discovery stories, etc. Just remember that posts are only as good as the stories that you are telling and the creative way you are telling them. **–Bryan Pieper, KNOCK**

Q: How consistent do you have to be with Snapchat or Instagram stories? What is your posting or planning strategy?

You need to be consistent, but that doesn't mean that you must do the same type of thing all of the time. Being able to fail and pivot and learn from that, is important but consistency is what you need in order to build fan engagement and naturally build brand ambassadors from fans. People engage with other people or brands based on triggers and these are usually emotional so find ways to emotionally connect with others. **–Josh Baird, FOX Sports**

When we talk about telling stories, telling a story isn't just a series of interconnected images that we are pushing out. Stories are something that requires planning. Consider, "What do we want to say? What is the narrative? How do we show the narrative?" I'm surprised that I don't see more creators doing storyboards ahead of time. Elevate your quality on Instagram and Snapchat before you start worrying about the quantity. **–Justin Celko, Blitz**

Engaging in the Inbox with Email Marketing

Here are some key takeaways from this topic:

- **Personalization is key**
  Create a one-on-one connection with your audience by building personal and customized email campaigns. Dive into your data to understand your audience and their behaviors.
- **Use social to learn from your customers**
  The best way to test content is to create a social post like a tweet or an Instagram post and gauge your audience's reaction. Listen to what your audience responds to on social and incorporate that into your email marketing.
- **Your emails should be about your users**
  Don't send emails that are brand-centric, instead keep your emails simple. Focus on what your audience needs and create email campaigns that offer value to your audience.

> **Watch these videos on our website:** Get these session videos delivered to your inbox by registering this book at MediaLeaders.com/dmt/videos/ (and be the first to hear about our next events).

Q: How do you engage in the inbox today with customization, personalization, and analytics?

We are seeing a lot of clients really try to get that one-to-one personalization as accurate as possible. We are also seeing a lot of clients start to really dig into their analytics. I think what tends to happen is that you have a lot of data and then you don't always know how to use it, and really figuring out what your business goals are and what data you have and kind of using that to drive your campaigns is really important. **–Elizabeth Jacobi, Javelin Agency**

Personalization and customization are very important. We take a human-centric approach at my company where it is all about understanding who you are talking to as humans, what their wants are and what their needs are while trying to do so on minimal information. **–Ronnie Kassiff,Inbound Marketing Consultant**

I think there are some good ways to learn more as a marketer and one of those ways is social. Use social as a way to learn more about your customers. It's a lot quicker to put out a social post, like a photo on Instagram, and see what kind of feedback you get. It can tell you what kind of content people are interested in and then you can deliver email content that matches. **–Justin Soni, IBM Marketing Cloud**

Q: What are the content practices that you guys are using or your customers are using today that are really working and resonating?

The number one rule of content, especially when it comes to email, is that no one cares about you. No one woke up at 6am and said, "I wish this company would send me some spam today." So, your email shouldn't be about you, it should be about your user: what your user wants, what your user needs, etc. The more specific you can be, the better your email will perform. When you start getting into that level of specificity, that is when data comes in. **–Anita Taylor, Hopscotch**

We have started to tell clients today that they should be coding and developing the email for the mobile device first and then for the desktop because most people today are on their mobile device constantly and that is how they are being connected. **–Elizabeth Jacobi, Javelin Agency**

Testing is extremely important. That is how you know that the approach you're taking is working. You can also modify what emails get sent based on click behavior. Based on click behavior and website visits, you can have the system do all of the work for you. So if they're clicking through "x" amount of emails that are targeted towards marketing, then you can put them down a marketing track. That way, instead of asking 12 questions on a form that people are not interested in filling out, you can figure out based on the information that you already have (which is based on behavior) what they are interested in and what their challenges likely are. Then you can send them relevant information. **–Ronnie Kassiff, Inbound Marketing Consultant**

Q: What brands out there are doing things really well and inspire you to be more creative with your inbox marketing strategies?

I always think that retail is the first one out of the gate with pretty much everything because they have bigger budgets, more resources, and they get more eyeballs. I like to follow bigger brands to see what they are doing because I know that they have the capabilities behind them so they are probably going to be testing a lot of different things with different technologies. Nike is a good example because if you buy a pair of Nike shoes that are customized, they will send you these updates every three days with this graph of how your shoe is being made and pictures of the process. It's a really engaging transactional email. It's very cool. It sounds goofy, but it gets a lot of engagement. **–Justin Soni, IBM Marketing Cloud**

Effective Email Marketing Tips for Brands

For brands who want to consistently build their fan base, nurture their existing customers and increase their conversions, email marketing provides a lot of opportunities. We reached out to 17 digital marketing experts and asked them to share their best email marketing tips for brands. From your very first cold-email to following up after a sale, these email marketing tips will help you take your email marketing efforts to the next level.

1. Provide unique value to your subscribers

Give your email list something special for being subscribed, something that they can't get by just reading your blog or website. Rather than sending quick emails that just forward people to your blog post, consider using long-form emails that provide unique value related to your product. Try to add value on top of your blog content and encourage your email list to respond to your emails with questions, and share the email with friends. Just be human and be available⋯ It's the most important thing you can do.
–Derric Haynie, Rebrandly

2. Acquiring prospect leads through email takes time

Acquiring customers via email has been proven to be a very viable marketing strategy for many online retailers. In order to boost your brand and acquire new customers, you must put your best foot forward. In order to get potential customers interested in your products, you must provide value. Showcase something compelling about your business or give an incredible deal to entice them to visit your website. Emails provide a very limited opportunity to showcase your brand message so remember to construct your message in an articulate and simple manner. Try to be creative with the subject lines.

The first email you send may not be viewed so don't be afraid to reestablish your brand with another email. Acquiring prospect leads with email takes time and a lot of people will not open the email until one of the subject lines resonates with them. Once they view your email message the conversion and click rates increase by over 50%. However, that does not mean spam will be an effective strategy, remember to limit your brand emails to 2-3 times per week. Nothing is more detrimental to a business than being associated with spam. When done in the correct manner, follow up emails are by far the most effective way to develop an authentic relationship with your new positional customers. **–Lisa Chu, Black n Bianco**

3. Focus on writing the best subject lines

Did you know that approximately 35% of email recipients open an email based on the subject line alone and that 69% of email recipients will report an email as spam solely based on the subject line? So, if you want higher conversion rates, more leads, loyal customers, and an above-average ROI on marketing efforts, you've got to be using the best email subject lines.

Starting out and writing cold emails? Less is more. The template that gave me my highest conversion rate had less than sixty words on it (signature included). The email should contain everything that will impress the recipient, help them understand what you must offer, and most importantly a call to action. Don't forget to consider how your email will look on mobile devices. **–George Schildge, Matrix Marketing Group**

4. Craft your emails with your customer in mind
The biggest mistake we were making with our emails was using company logic as opposed to customer logic. You really need to put yourself in the mind of your customer when crafting your emails. Run your email copy by friends and get feedback.

Then, split your email up:
- Write captivating subject lines to increase your open rate
- Tease your product or service in the sub-head to peak curiosity
- Utilize the header to convert your subscriber's curiosity into interest

In the body of the email quickly point out how you are helping your subscriber
Finish with a CTA (call-to-action) that gets your subscribers on your landing page

The goal of your email should be to achieve a high click-through-rate. Do not try to make or close a sale in your email. **–Bryan Clayton, GreenPal**

5. Create a lifecycle campaign
The most essential and effective way to engage your customers via email is to create a lifecycle campaign. A lifecycle campaign contains different mailings; they are sent out at different times, so as to follow customers along their

journey. If you are in the travel industry, for example: send a thank you email after a purchase, tips about the destination city two weeks before departure; weather forecast 3 days before departure; a survey when the trip is over. It's important to communicate with your customers whenever it is necessary so that you can gradually nurture them. – **Haley Gong, Webpower Asia**

6. Be simple, clear and helpful

We email everybody who uses our pet insurance quote system and opts in for email follow ups. We've tested every different type of email campaign, template, etc. What we've found that has the best response rate and best results are being simple, clear and helpful.

For example, don't bombard people with sales pitches, but instead say, "Hey, let us know how we can help you." Ensure that your emails aren't sent from a generic address, this will create goodwill and allow you to learn about your customers' needs. **–Nick Braun, PetInsuranceQuotes.com**

7. Ask for customer feedback

One email hack that has been successful for us is a re-engagement effort. Using data, we were able to create a campaign to reach out to users who hadn't used our software in several months. We asked them a one-question poll: Why not? Not only were we able to get useful feedback from past users, but those who participated received a discount on their next purchase. Our email campaign was a win-win, and highly successful. **–Kim Kohatsu, Charles Ave Marketing**

8. Use humor to grab your customer's attention

Humor is a great way to instantly connect with people and get their attention. Sending a funny email an excellent way to stand out from the many other emails your customers receive daily.

Below is an example of one of my most successful emails:

Hello Jenny,

I tried to contact you regarding Blu Skin Care's amazing Valentine's Day skin care sale and haven't heard back. Let me know if:

You're interested but will respond within the next few days.

You received my emails but aren't interested right now so I should stop emailing you because frankly, you're annoyed.

I should follow up in a few months.

You're too busy playing with your kitten to care about skin care right now.

Zondra Wilson

–Zondra Wilson, Blu Skin Care

9. Understand email frequency, cadence, and unsubscribing

The best email marketing tip I can provide is to make sure you have a great understanding of email cadence, frequency, and what cause users to unsubscribe. If you know how often you can reach out to your audience without them unsubscribing, you can maximize your campaigns. There is a point where too many emails cause a large number of potential customers to unsubscribe and unless you are operating exactly at the perfect frequency, there is an opportunity to improve.

Cadence, on the other hand, is more about the pattern of your emails. No one wants or will even open a promotional email that is sent out in the middle of the night. The best time to grab someone's attention is when they are already in their inbox, which usually happens sometime after work and before dinner. If your emails are sent in the right pattern at the right time of the day, you are far more likely to get the attention of the end user. **–Sam Wheeler, Inseev Interactive**

10. Include social deals in your CTA

Include a social deal in one or more of your call to actions on every email campaign geared towards new customers. Modern consumers, especially millennials, love to purchase social deals with their friends. In an email marketing campaign, a call to action that includes 'a friend' is more likely to be forwarded and purchased with a group of potential customers.

You must be careful with how you word this call to action. The best way to go about crafting this is to write a call to action that connects with a basic 'Social Deal' landing page on your site that a potential customer can share with others. This not only helps to drive more traffic to your site but can also help with link building and SEO. **–Wesley Flippo, Buy the Best Drone**

11. Avoid flashy email marketing tricks

One of the more successful email marketing tips that I've seen recently is the email campaigns that deliberately don't look like marketing emails. They present themselves in more or less plain text, include a couple of links, and then they sign off. These non-marketing type emails are very simple, personal and obviously effective. They're not trying to sell too hard and surprisingly that gets a lot more clicks than any flashy email marketing tips. **–Abbey Brown, FM Outsource**

12. Start a conversation

The number one email marketing tip businesses need to think about when using email is to create a dialogue with the other person. Typically, if someone has signed up to something, you'll try and sell to them instantly, but that person isn't ready to buy. It's important to build a relationship with your subscriber, and the only way to do that is to provide value and by starting a conversation. **– Gavin Bell, Blue Cliff Media**

13. Resend the same email to everyone who didn't open it the first time

At SuperOffice, we've built resending the same email a second time into our email marketing program. The way it works is simple: Send an email campaign to your email list, as per usual. Then, 24 hours later, create a second campaign, but remove everyone who opened the email the first time, and resend it to your list using a slightly modified subject line.

It's one of the quickest and easiest email marketing tips, and not only do you reach the people that missed your first email, but you can also double the amount of opens and clicks you get for your email campaign! **–Steven Macdonald, SuperOffice**

14. Get to know your audience

Get to know your audience, learn to understand what they like and how they behave on the Internet. Write attractive and short subject lines. The longer your subject lines are, the more likely it is that people won't click on your emails. Be brief and to the point right from the first sentence. Nobody opens emails to read thorough reports or intricate articles. Start to create your emails based on prospect's previous behavior. Analyze how people have interacted with your emails in the past to know how to do it better the next time! Lastly, be creative and innovative. Thinking out of the box will pay off. **–Alexander Grosu, inSegment**

15. Unsubscribe passive leads

No doubt leads are vital for your business. However, in reality, some of the leads are completely passive. They never open emails and don't interact with you at all. So, we can't expect any purchases from them. Having 5,000 high-quality leads is much more powerful than having 50,000 passive leads.

Track when someone does not open your emails for a while and then send an email that notifies them that you will not bother them anymore. Like this one:

We noticed you haven't opened our evening sales emails in a while, so we have gone ahead and opted you out of them. We don't want to clutter your inbox anymore.

Click here to opt back in or to change your email preferences.

It's an effective technique because it shows you care about people. If your customer is no longer interested in the brand, this email leaves them with a good impression. If your customer is still interested but was unable to open the emails for some reason, the email will make them like and trust your brand even more. **–Jason Roberts, My Handyman Services**

16. Advertise your email campaign as a mini course

When soliciting email addresses on your website, advertise your email campaign as a 'six-part mini course.' Consumers are much more intrigued by a 'course,' which promises useful information, and specifying the number of installments tells potential customers what to expect. Focus on excellent content for the first six editions with the occasional soft sell, and then go for the sale on the seventh email with a hard sell. Make the hard sell simply irresistible by throwing in a bonus, such as a free sample, trial period or e-book. **–Simon Slade, Doubledot Media**

17. Bloggers & Podcasters: Nurture subscribers by sending weekly media leads

The one trick I use to nurture leads and engage with prospects via e-mail is sending weekly media leads. This trick can work for anyone who has a blog or podcast. Essentially, I send out a topic list/editorial calendar of what I'll be writing on or reporting on over the coming weeks and give my opt-in list the first crack at weighing in. It gives them the opportunity to get noticed and really participate in the conversation. **–Blair Nicole, Media Moguls PR**

Tips to Optimize Email Subject Lines

If you've ever launched an email marketing campaign, you know the challenge of crafting subject lines, and how difficult it can be to increase your open rates. With open rates having such a direct impact on the success of your campaign, ensure that you are optimizing every email subject line.

We found several email marketing experts to share some of their best subject line tips.

1. Think about how your market will interact with your emails

One of the key missteps I see companies, clients and students make when it comes to email marketing is not paying enough attention to the subject line. The most creative and clever email content in the world can never achieve results if prospects don't first open your email! They'll never see the brilliant prose you created if your email subject line does not compel them to take that first step toward a purchase decision—a click to open your email.

To help connect effectively with prospects through email marketing, marketers need to think about how their market will be interacting with their email based on where they are, and what they're likely to be doing when they see your message. If they're in a B2B environment, they're thinking business and likely juggling a myriad of different tasks. They're probably most attentive to internal messages from their managers, their colleagues, and their customers. In a B2C environment, you're competing with social messages from friends and acquaintances.

Think about how an email is received in terms of the way you handle your own email interactions. In order for your email to earn a click, it needs to be compelling both in terms of who it came from and what the implied or, better yet, the explicit, benefit to them may be. It's critical that email marketers put themselves inside the heads of their target audience and really think carefully about how to deliver a benefit that's likely to be better than what all of their other emails have to offer! **–Linda Pophal, Strategic Communications**

2. Analyze the effectiveness of your email subject lines

When it comes to email pitching, it is all about the subject line. When I'm pitching an article for coverage, I include the brand name and representative in the subject line. This way, the editor knows that I'm reaching out on behalf of a reputable company or CEO and will think opening the email is more worth their time. Editors are flooded with emails and leaving a generic subject line is the quickest way to get ignored. I'd recommend using a plugin to track opens of emails, as well, so that you can analyze the effectiveness of your email subject lines. Pitching really comes down to trial and error and it takes a bit to figure out where the sweet spot is. Taking that extra time to research your subject line will help tremendously in your pitching efforts.

Of course, the pitch itself in the body of the email needs to be worth the open too. Stay away from misleading email subject lines since this will just irritate the recipient. **–Amber Whiteside, Main Path Marketing**

3. Offer something without the intention of making a sale

It depends on the type of email you're sending, but when you sent out cold prospecting emails, let them know right away what you're doing. Tricking someone into opening your emails with a cheeky subject line may improve your open rates, but that probably won't lead to a higher number of clicks. Because of this, I have my subject line: "Hi (First Name), coming in ice-cold with a follow-up to Garrett's (our CEOs) emails." It's a creative, catchy opening line that references previous emails we've sent, but also lets them know right away that they haven't heard from me specifically before. We then offer a free high-level audit of their current marketing campaigns. Offering something without the intention of making a sale works really well, especially because once they agree to our free audit, and see the level of work we provide, they're already interested! **–Andrew Choco, Directive Consulting**

4. Grab your recipient's attention

No matter what's inside the email, I always make sure that the subject line I select is catchy enough to grab recipient's attention in the first place. For example, when I am pitching to a client who I would need to hear back from, my subject line would be something like "What do you think?". Short, meaningful and catchy email subject lines are a great way to increase the open rate for your email marketing campaigns. **–Aqib Nazir, AqibNazir.com**

5. Save your recipient time

It's pretty simple. When I compose an email, in the title, I always format it in the following manner: "Hi Sam | Quick Question About Email Pitches"

By putting the name in the title, it adds personalization. By saying, Quick Question it is somewhat intriguing and the person knows it won't take much time to read. Including the subject at the end of the title shows the person what you are looking to talk about, which if you do your research, should be relevant to him or her. **–Jason Parks, The Media Captain**

6. Create a template you can personalize
Create a template that appears to be an original email with blank spaces for you to personalize the email with the recipient's name, email address, and subject line. It's tedious, but in the case of query letters to editors, for example, they certainly don't want to feel like you are querying everyone else. **–William Seavey, Author**

7. Pose a question
We may be told not to judge a book by its cover, but we most definitely judge an email by its subject line. The subject line is the first thing to grab our attention, so it's crucial for it to leave the reader wanting more. One great trick is to pose a question to your audience. This allows for your email to become an engaging conversation rather than a boring message. At The Halo Group, a branding and marketing communications agency based in the heart of Manhattan, we experiment with creative email subject lines and, through A/B testing, in order to ultimately decide which subject line performs best. **–Linda Passante, The Halo Group**

8. Shorter email subject lines get opened at a higher rate

Write a clear, compelling subject line that tells what your email is about. Craft it so it's in the best interest of the recipient to open your email. Shorter email subject lines tend to perform better because they stand out. Multiple research studies show shorter subject lines get opened at a higher rate because friends and family write short subject lines. People's brains scan for shorter email subject lines. Finally, six lines or less is a fantastic guideline for the body of your email. Keeping your emails short is especially important when pitching a blogger or journalist because they're busy. If they see a wall of text, they won't read it. – **Clint Evans, StandOut Authority**

9. Experiment with interesting subject lines

Unusual subject lines get read. The subject will either pull the receiver in or have them pressing the delete button before they even see the email. Take your most interesting, quotable line and put it in the subject. You want something that intrigues and leaves the person wanting more. Questions are effective too. Leave your audience thinking. – **Michelle Hutchison, Finder**

10. Use humorous email subject lines

When trying to get someone to open your email, nothing stands out more than something funny in the subject line. What the subject line does is get them to open your email and that is the hardest part. If you can convert them on the subject line, you have won. **–Gene Caballero, GreenPal**

Digital Outreach to Get Positive PR

Here are some key takeaways from this topic:

- **Incorporate multimedia in your PR**
  Images, infographics and video capture the attention of media outlets and make their job easier.
- **Know your audience**
  Don't just blast a release far and wide and see what sticks. If you know the audience and reporters you need to reach, target your efforts there.
- **Find out where your message is resonating geographically**
  You might be surprised to find shares coming from parts of the country you weren't directly targeting, representing a new growth opportunity.
- **Be creative in your messaging**
  Just because you have something to pitch or sell doesn't make it newsworthy, but if your message is creative and elicits some kind of emotional response, you'll be more successful.

> **Watch these videos on our website:** Get these session videos delivered to your inbox by registering this book at MediaLeaders.com/dmt/videos/ (and be the first to hear about our next events).

Q: What are the best practices when it comes to using digital means to promote or initiate public relations?

We advocate for companies to have multimedia within their press releases and to make sure that they are interactive. – **Victoria Green, Business Wire**

Analysis. Analyze your purpose and understand who your audience is and who you want to read or watch your materials. **–Curtis Boyd, Future Solutions Media**

You can't activate everybody. You must start with smaller groups so that you can really target to activate those audiences. Also, be sure to activate through a marriage of text and multimedia, because only 37% of the world enjoys reading text. **–Serena Ehrlich, Business Wire**

Q: When you are talking about digital PR + traditional PR, what tools are you using?

We use the databases like Cision and Groupie, and we dive into the SEO tools such as seoClarity and Moz. Moz actually allows us to look at our competition and see what some of their major wins are, what their backlinks are, and what people are talking about with regard to that competitor as well as look at the editors that are covering that particular topic to see if we can add them to our media list. You can also see where your competitors are not focusing and get a very raw picture to help you build your strategy. **–Kate Lobel, Power Digital Marketing**

We have quite a few tools that I like right now, but the first one is Contently.com. They help connect brands to writers, and what I like about them is that they can give us access to tremendous writers who can do anything from blog writing to investigative journalism. We also really love Ceros, which is a New York company that helps us take white papers and other material and turn it into animated gifs and videos. **– Ben Plomion, GumGum**

Q: What about more traditional services?

We want our clients on the publication that caters to our audience, so using places like Muck Rack we will develop a list of writers that will be a good fit for us. I start following them, build up a rapport with them, and then pitch to them. These large databases can help you narrow down your search and figure out who can help get you or your client's message onto these larger publications. **–Curtis Boyd, Future Solutions Media**

Know your goal. We frequently hear people say, "The *Wall Street Journal*–it has got to be the *Wall Street Journal*." We ask why and they say, "Sales," but the *Wall Street Journal* might not be the best place to drive sales. So, one of the things that you can do through these databases is actually pull lists for every goal and then customize your outreaches to those goals and to those publications. **–Serena Ehrlich, Business Wire**

Q: What about when you are actually looking to distribute your news or looking for a bigger platform? What do you see as far as reach amplification?

Our advice is to use multimedia with your distribution efforts, to know your audience, and to avoid blasting everyone. Knowing who you are sending news to, knowing their audience and the reporters you are trying to reach is important. **–Victoria Green, Business Wire**

I also like using pay-as-you-go ad network platforms like Outbrain or dlvr.it. They are completely online, and you can take a news release (and we include this in our distribution) and it gets put into an ad block. You get to tell them who your target audience is, and then these platforms match your content with articles on the web in order to hopefully get people to open your article.

I have done major Outbrain campaigns that have failed and I wasn't charged any money, and I have done major Outbrain campaigns that have succeeded and cost me $23.

So, they are not expensive, but they do help you get that news visibility that you want. **–Serena Ehrlich, Business Wire**

Outbrain can charge as low as $0.03 per 1,000 impressions, which is a really good deal. If your content matches, you have an enticing title and imagery that really connects, then you are going to get a tremendous amount of visibility on places like Outbrain. **–Curtis Boyd, Future Solutions Media**

You don't want to be the *National Enquirer* of headlines, the clickbait (definition: Outlandish headlines crafted for the sole purpose of driving clicks.) of headlines, but when it comes to getting people to see your news it really dials down to your headline and your multimedia asset. **–Serena Ehrlich, Business Wire**

Q: Who is doing it right? What brands have you seen that are demonstrating strong programming?

Essentia Mattress. Based out of Canada, they are the leader in organic and natural memory foam mattresses. What they are doing is really integrating every single digital channel as much as possible ranging from SEO, web development, PPC, PR, social media, etc. **–Kate Lobel, Power Digital Marketing**

Miller Lite asked us to find images posted of Miller Lite because they realized that a lot of images did not have any hashtags or text posted with it, and their social listening tools cannot listen for images or video. They hired us to help them use image recognition to scan those images on Twitter, Instagram, Tumblr and Facebook to find images that are related to the brand. They then used those images to generate marketing insight and create a new marketing campaign. **–Ben Plomion, GumGum**

Q: How do you measure social PR/digital communications programs?

UTM codes and being able to track goes directly into Google Analytics, and as a traditional PR person, I was freaked out by diving into analytics, but now it is my best friend because it gives you so much insight. Even just registering your client on the backend can show you how many sessions were brought to your client's website from that specific placement. You can also see how long someone stays on your site from the first placement and most importantly if they actually converted. **–Kate Lobel, Power Digital Marketing**

Q: There is this concept in PR that the number one metric is coverage. What do you see as other metrics that can come out now that there are more analytics available?

We have a lot of integrated analytics tools where within 24 hours of a news release going out, you can go in and see the data, the impressions, who tweeted it, etc. There are so many metrics we offer that come with the cost of distributing your release, and many people do not look at these as much as they should. **–Victoria Green, Business Wire**

One of the top metrics that we are now seeing is georesonance–this concept that you can now track where your information is resonating. So, if you are a California-based program and you see a high number of shares coming from Texas, that gives you three major pieces of action:

1) You call Texas media market outlets and try to set up an interview with your customer because conversations are coming.

2) You do social marketing.

3) You tell your sales teams that you have activity in these markets. **–Serena Ehrlich, Business Wire**

Q: What advice do you have regarding the future of digital tools?

I feel like videos and graphics are becoming more and more of a part of modern publication and capturing attention for readership. Social media will intermesh even more with major publications as more and more people spend time on social media, so I think the future is more visual and more social than we might want it to be. **–Curtis Boyd, Future Solutions Media**

One of the first things you learn in PR is to ask 'Is this newsworthy?' I think people forget that. They get lost in their message and trying to sell, and some people just do not care. You need to get more on the creative side of things and be creative in your release. **–Victoria Green, Business Wire**

Q: Are you seeing that across the board press releases do need to start integrating graphics, or does it really depend on the audience?

I think it depends on the audience but it is not necessarily graphics. Multimedia, yes. Multimedia meaning infographics, video, and interactive elements like pictures that show before/after images. **–Victoria Green, Business Wire**

The biggest complainers to us about companies not using multimedia are TV and radio. These radio stations and TV stations have websites, and no news is on the web without an image. **–Serena Ehrlich, Business Wire**

Best Practices in PR, Search and Social

Presented by:
Serena Ehrlich, Director of Social and Evolving Media for Business Wire
Here are some key takeaways from this topic:

- **Consumers place a high level of trust in editorial content over paid placement** Learn the best strategies for getting media outlets to cover your brand by giving them easy access to informative stats, good quotes and strong visuals so they can produce quality content quickly.
- **Make your news relevant to trending topics**
  Use tools like Google Trends to find out what topics people are talking about today, this week or this month, and tweak your press releases to create tie-ins.
- **Learn the best tactical tips for each social media platform you use**
  On LinkedIn, give users hard news that will make them feel well-informed. On Facebook, tailor your posts to fit different demographics. Take longer videos you've put on YouTube and find clever ways to condense them for Vine. Every site has its own insider tips if you do your research.

1. Understand the needs of today's media

When it comes to creating content that (a) people will notice and (b) will move them through the sales and marketing funnel, editorial coverage hands down is the most trusted piece of content someone can generate. 67% of consumers trust editorial content.

If this coverage is shared by a third party through search/social, the numbers show that trust goes up even higher. 84% of consumer's trust earned media/word of mouth. So, company communications start with getting editorial coverage, but it's going to be the flow of that editorial coverage across social and search that makes a real difference.

When Business Wire asked reporters, "What is your number one metric for success?", the top three answers were page views, social media sharing and the number of visits to the site. So, when I send out an email pitching a story promoting Business Wire, I include the sentence "If you are able to write about this, I will share this through Business Wire's news amplification program." That means I'll put it on Twitter, put it in Reddit if it's relevant, and put in on Business Wire's Intranet (and giving my 500-person company multiple choices of how they want to share it). So "news amplification" is just me seeding it out–things we're all doing anyway. And if you take those actions, the next time you pitch them you'll get "Yes," because they know that you will meet their metrics. By the way, if you don't, they're less likely to write about you next time.

Here's another tip: Reporters are under a lot of pressure to produce content quickly–so don't just pitch them; provide them what they need to write a good story. Give them data, because people love data. Give them a photo or multimedia. Give them great quotes. Give them links to places on your website where they can get the backup information. Make it easy for them. Add that you're going to share their story out for them, and you're their best friend.

2. Craft a better news release
Here are a couple of tricks when it comes to effective press releases:

- **You need keywords in your headlines to make it stand out.** Think about the news you want to pitch and ask, how does this impact common themes that are being written about right now in my top publications? If you can identify key phrases that are really hot right now in your media space–say, Internet of Things–you can go into Google Trends, put those terms in, and it's going to tell you the search volume. The higher the search volume, the more relevant the topic, and the more likely your release is to be opened.

- **The other thing you can do–nobody knows about this–is use Google Suggest**, which is just Google's autocomplete function for searches. Open a clean browser and start typing in your company name, and Google will start auto-suggesting statements. You will see the top searches that people are doing right now based on the company name you put in. So, let's say you're at an agency and you're pitching Bank of America–you can type in Bank of America and see what pops up. This tells you the most common questions people have about this company and what they are searching for related to this company, and you can use it to create pitch angles.

- **Focus on headlines, subheads, and first sentences.** When you write a news release, blog post or anything else you're publishing, reporters see your headline and your first sentence. It needs to be really strong, so when it appears with your headline, it increases open rates. Your only SEO opportunities to get your content seen and opened are in the headlines, subheads, and multimedia assets–nothing else.

3. Add visuals
Visuals trigger interest, emotion and engagement with your reader. They also give a reporter or social media user value-added interest they'll want to share or use in a story.

You want to use a visual when:
- When you want ROI
- When you have a complicated story
- When you want to build an emotional relationship
- When you want visibility, engagement, earnings
- When you have new offices, new products, new partnerships
- Whenever you get a chance

4. Start using URL builders
Using trackable URLs is key to tracking your campaigns. Any analytics program will have a URL builder, and you really want this for news releases, social channels, blogs, and email. All you have to do is fill out the relevant information on your URL builder, and you get a long URL. You can use it to track the number of people who clicked and went in and what they're doing when they get there. It's only a snapshot, because a lot of people won't click the link; they'll just Google your headline or company name and go in that way. It's valuable information that you can use to improve the success of your press releases. By doing this you are using

UTM links to drive measurable ROI.

5. Learn the insider tricks for using social media to your advantage

Search engines and social media platforms love news, and they love helping you share it. Why? Their users demand it, because today's audience researches absolutely everything, because it's so easy to do with a mobile device always on hand.

Search and social are spaces that are always changing, but the key point to remember is that search engines and social platforms love your news content. Their users are constantly researching everything, so they demand access to quality editorial wherever they are. So how do you get your brand's news on these channels?

a.) **Google.** Google does a huge amount of research on what people are looking for online. What are people looking for? Web sites, social properties, and news. So, when you search on Google, those are your top results.

If you go into Google and search a company name, there's a note that says "Click here for more stories." That takes you to Google News, and here's all your coverage in one spot. What's great is that here is also your press release, because Google knows people are also interested in the sources. This is Google serving up the work you're doing and putting it at the top of search. Just remember to try and keep it relevant to the current topics people are searching for.

b.) **LinkedIn.** LinkedIn likes to give its readers news that make them feel informed. That's why they are scraping news releases as well as articles on the web. If you are a quoted source in a press release or the contact of a news release, LinkedIn will scrape that and send it to all of your contacts. Right now, we frequently use CEOs as the quoted sources, but if you work for a B2B company, try this: quote your head of sales. Why? Because every person and every prospect that your salesperson is connected to will get this.

c.) **Twitter.** The typical Twitter user's aspiration is to be the first, the smartest, or the funniest. So, here's a tip: If you have a news story going out this morning and it contains a statistic, don't tweet the headline first. Tweet the stat instead–that way, readers feel they have valuable information before they've even gotten out of bed. Also, promote any coverage you secure or content you create a minimum of 15 times, scheduled out over three or four days. It's going to do two things: One, every time you Tweet, you're initiating someone else to retweet it for you and advocate. Two, you're sending more people to the media site that wrote the story, which makes the reporter happy, because you're helping them meet their metric. Separately, there's a free service called Click to Tweet. It lets you pre-write a tweet, add in hashtags and your URL, and then you just put a call to action right into your news release or blog post and say, "Tweet this." This works especially well when you do it after bullet points, especially if it's stats, because people love data. It's amazing. People love to share and look smart. Make sure that you also drive them back to your website at the end.

d.) **Facebook.** Facebook shows content to different users based on their preferences and demographics–so make sure every update caters to different audiences, even if the link is the same. So, if I put out a whitepaper on "Best Practices in PR," I could tell younger readers, *learn everything you need to know to be as smart as your boss.* But for older audiences

I could say, *Get up to speed on digital as fast as possible.* If I tailor a post to a certain demographic, Facebook will only show that post to people who meet these demographics.

e.) **Instagram.** Instagram is not the world's greatest place to put news articles because at this point they don't have inbound traffic options. But we are seeing a lot of companies utilizing Instagram to support events, product, and even their employees. GE, IBM, and these types of companies will do these things called "View from my desk" where internally they ask people to share views from their day at work. They get great content that shows what it is like to work in their office, and their employees get validation. They're also going to like and/or share it–and When employees share something out, they're advocating about your business to their personal audience.

f.) **Pinterest.** Everyone tells me, "I don't use Pinterest for work. Pinterest is the wedding site." That's completely incorrect, especially for B2B. This is probably one of the single best platforms. But remember this: One of the worst mistakes you can make on Pinterest is to not put the URL behind a photo. You don't want someone to click a photo only to see a bigger photo come up. You get no inbound traffic. The reason why we don't see Pinterest in our analytics is because of that scenario.

g.) **YouTube.** Almost 33% of all searches on YouTube right now are for news. YouTube, Huffington Post Video, and Yahoo Video are the top three news sites for video. For those who say they don't want to create YouTube videos because they don't want to fight the existing SEO on YouTube, consider short video products. If you can say something in a shorter format, do it. Brands have had great success by going through their best longer videos, finding the ones that generate the most views and turning them into six-second videos. It's easy to do, and it makes them more accessible.

Social Media Tips for Reputation Management

We've been hearing about the importance of word-of-mouth marketing since the advent of commerce itself, and it remains as valuable as ever. The difference is that today the conversation has moved online, and what customers say and hear about your brand on social media can make or break your brand reputation.

We caught up with 4 marketing experts to explore how brands use social media to improve their reputation management, online marketing, and search engine rankings.

Q: What are your best tips to help a business with their reputation management online? How do brands develop an awesome online reputation by keeping people engaged?

It's part of human nature to be critical–or at least more critical–towards people you don't have a relationship or any direct involvement with. Social media, as an engagement platform, allows you to have more direct involvement with your audience, customers, and people who are interested in what you do and say. When you're engaged online, you'll find that people have a less critical attitude in general toward your brand or company.

At the same time, if there is a legitimate concern, you have a better opportunity to reach out in a friendlier way and have a manageable level of discourse rather than having to deal with the trolls who are just there to bash people. The people who have a connection with you will reach out to you more as a friend than rather than, 'Hey, I have a complaint, and I'm going to trash you because I don't know who you are.' So, maintaining your engagement online really helps. **–Stoney deGeyter, Pole Position Marketing**

Q: How can a brand be proactive in overcoming any negative feedback online?

Our biggest strategy, which has worked amazingly well for us, is to be extremely consistent with how we handle any negativity via social media. For instance, whenever someone has an issue, comment or question, we always respond very quickly and with the same answer. If they have an issue with a product, we acknowledge it and say, 'Send us an email, and we'll get this replaced.' So then when someone new comes into the social media space with an issue, our fans are already there, and they already know how we respond. They will even respond to us and say, 'Hey, this doesn't sound like Lot801. You should send them an email, and they'll probably replace it for you.' So, having a community that's already there for us builds trust and helps create a positive brand reputation for us. **–Lindsay White, Lot801 Marketing**

Q: What are the important tactical tips for what we can do on a daily or weekly basis to monitor our accounts?

For small–to medium-sized businesses, I think the biggest thing is to have a dedicated person for this, whether it's someone in-house or somebody like me who is a social media manager. This person acts as a community manager to 'listen' online, look at what happens on Twitter, put out a Google Alert on the company name or variations of the name, and so on. They should then be able to respond to the business owner, who is busy running the business itself. If they don't allocate any marketing money or a dedicated person to that, it can very quickly escalate into a bad situation when a bad review comes in or somebody starts bashing a product or service on the Facebook page, for example. So, the fact somebody is there monitoring and listening is very important.

With Google Alerts, you can get them sent to you as soon as an alert comes in. I have it sent to me in digest form once a day. Meanwhile, for businesses, I think if you Google your business name, you want to do it as often as once a week and make sure you're incognito.

I do this with my own children as well, because I have some teens going off to college. It's personal branding as well as business branding, so make sure you're Googling your own name, too. **–Dorien Morin, More in Media**

Q: What do you tell brands that think they can just avoid the web altogether?

The problem is that whether you are on the web or not, your audience is. So, if you're not there, they're still going to write reviews about your products or say things about your brand name or your business. And if you're not there, you're basically just letting it go without addressing it.

The chatter is going to happen. The best opportunity is for you to also be there so you can work with that, whether it's cleaning up messes that you see people are posting about or just engaging with your audience to build that relationship. You don't want to create a situation where people are talking about you and you're not paying attention. Nobody likes to talk when nobody's listening– they'll go to brands that are listening. **–Stoney deGeyter, Pole Position Marketing**

Q: What are your top two favorite networks to build a community of awesome fans?

Instagram absolutely hands-down, especially now that they have video content. Video content is going to be the biggest thing this year along with visual content in general. While Facebook is always top of the list, Instagram is pretty close to Facebook if not overpassing it. **–Lindsay White, Lot801 Marketing**

Q: Which online marketing tips would you teach a small business to earn good brand reputation online?

Create a bunch of social profiles. A lot of small businesses that I find are only on Facebook, so I always explain to them that if they make a Pinterest account, a LinkedIn page, and an Instagram account, those become ranked in search engines very quickly. So, that's one fast way to do it. And then getting some PR through stories written about them helps too. But a quick, basically free way to do it get a bunch of social media profiles, fill them out with the keywords, and that very quickly ranks you. **–Dorien Morin, More in Media**

Q: What tools do you use to monitor your online reputation?

There is a tool I developed with my staff that can help, too. Dorien mentioned searching for your name and variations of your name–sometimes first and last plus the city you're in or the school your student goes to or whatever helps identify you–but doing that every day or every other day can get exhausting. So, we've tried to make it easier with a tool called FootprintFridayReport.com.

Every Friday morning it emails you part of our newsletter including a Google-assisted email with all the buttons you want to fill in to help manage your brand presence and brand reputation. It goes to Google, and you can see the Google results that your customers, clients or those that want to work with your brand would see. **–Josh Ochs, Media Leaders**

Q: How can a social media policy help organizations manage their online results?

It is very important for organizations to have a social media policy to establish how the business interacts with people online. There need to be very clear expectations for anyone who's going to represent your company on social media. Also, keep your social-media policy up to date, making sure employees are educated on the newest programs and social networking sites and how your policy applies.

Otherwise, you take the risk of compromised productivity, brand reputation damage, data loss or employee behavior that doesn't represent your company values. Any of these cases can lead to monetary or reputation loss, and even regulatory compliance fines depending on the industry you're in. **–Dr. Bennet Hammer, Hammer IT Consulting**

Ad Spend: PPC & Retargeting

Here are some key takeaways from this topic:

- **PPC is a cost model and retargeting is a tactic**
  PPC means pay-per-click and retargeting is a strategy where a brand can use ads to re-engage with people who have already bought a product from thee brand or are interested in buying.
- **Retargeting should have a higher conversion rate**
  Since retargeted ads go to customers who have already purchased or are interested in purchasing from you then the chances of that customer converting is much higher.
- **Add captions to your video ads**
  Only 30% of Facebook videos have sounds so it's important to include captions in your video ads. Adding captions to your videos has a chance of increasing your CTR and overall conversion rate.

Watch these videos on our website: Get these session videos delivered to your inbox by registering this book at MediaLeaders.com/dmt/videos/ (and be the first to hear about our next events).

Q: What is PPC and retargeting? Is one better than the other?

PPC can be retargeting. In AdWords', for instance, you can do retargeting campaigns where you are paying per click and usually it's more of a combined technique. You use both PPC and retargeting. You have your PPC campaigns to attract new customers and you have your retargeting campaigns to re-engage the ones who have already bought or who have an interest in buying. **–Mark Williams, Fullscreen**

I do come across a lot of smaller companies who are using search as their only tactic but search is only a small part of the customer journey. You have to also think about retargeting, but what are you retargeting with? Yes, there can be search retargeting but there can also be visual retargeting. You can literally retarget with television ads. **– Allen Martinez, Noble Digital**

PPC is a cost model, retargeting is a tactic. Retargeting can also be run on a CPM, it's what works best for your brand. If you are layering on the best smart data to retarget, you might be more efficient doing that on a CPM because you are not paying for the click so it is really testing out different platforms and different models, to find the ones that work for you. **–Rachel Klausner, OpenSlate**

Q: What is a good rule of thumb in terms of the amount that should be spent on retargeting vs other tactics?

Retargeting should convert a lot better than your prospecting campaigns (prospecting campaigns are driving new users into your funnel), so I always like to spend as much money as humanly possible with keeping the current conversion rate on remarketing and hopefully that is more than less. **–Steve Weiss, MuteSix**

Q: What are some creative techniques that you use or have seen?

A little trick that we do is to export all of the posts from Facebook and then reupload every single post through XML back into Facebook and you can put $ budgets against each post. Then the one post that gets the lowest cost per click will turn everything off. It's a really quick unique way to test every single post that you have to your website without spending a lot of money. **–Steve Weiss, MuteSix**

Remarketing can also be used to remarket an audience like viewers of a brand's YouTube channel. Similar to the sequential messaging Mark was referencing earlier about film trailers. If you can drive an audience anywhere, you want to market to people that are already fans of your brand, whether or not they have visited your site. You can actually place that remarketing pixel from your YouTube channel audience vs. from your website. This provides a different perspective and more unique remarketing pool than only looking at people cookied on your site. **–Rachel Klausner, OpenSlate**

One of our big techniques has been, aside from CRM data, is using third-parties. Now with AdWords' and with Facebook, they have opened up to allow third-party segment lists to come in. So, I am doing that with AdWords' and with Facebook Ad Manager where I bring in those lists to hit a certain demographic, a certain age, etc. **–Mark Williams, Fullscreen**

I still see a lot of people marketing video without adding captions to the videos. Only 30% of Facebook videos actually have sound to them so one key piece of advice I would give to everyone is to add captions to your videos. No one is going to listen to your video because the sound isn't on. Adding captions to your videos could actually increase your CTR and overall conversion rate. We integrate with Marketo for a couple of our clients where they build custom audiences based on users who actually open up your email, who engage and click over so if you have a large email list, you could do this manually as well, but you can take all of those users who have clicked and take that into Facebook as a custom audience. **–Steve Weiss, MuteSix**

Audience Q: How do you know whether the impressions you have are going to the right people when the campaign is a brand awareness campaign?

When you are running a brand awareness campaign, what you want is for people to start doing brand searches on Google and so the way to measure that is to look at the month-over-month differences in brand searches from your ads on Facebook, but you could also look at the actual engagements with the ad units. So, you could go on Facebook, read the comments and look at the shares as well as the conversions that might be coming from that brand awareness campaign. **–Steve Weiss, MuteSix**

A brand advertiser is also going to put importance on different success metrics. Marketers running brand

awareness campaigns are not necessarily looking at how many people went to the site and bought something as a result of the ad impression. They are looking at how engaged the viewers were with their message and if it resonated. Did they watch my full video? What was the ratio of people who skipped it vs. the ones who watched it? Did they remember my brand? Would they refer my brand to their friends? There are measurement tools out there from companies like Millward Brown to assess the success of these more "intangible" metrics, as well as free studies that Google will actually offer on brand lift, ad recall and more.–
Rachel Klausner, OpenSlate

Social Media Listening Tools

Here are some key takeaways from this panel:

- **Understand what inspires your audience to post on social**
  Tapping into your audiences' authentic experiences with your products and understanding how that inspires them to share that moment on social can be used to structure your product strategy.
- **Utilize your Facebook audience**
  Most social platforms don't allow you to customize your messaging based on who is reading your post, except Facebook. Facebook allows you to segment your audience and create optimized messages for each segment. Implementing this strategy can give you an advantage since many brands aren't utilizing this feature yet.
- **Establish your goals**
  Having a clear understanding of your goals will make it easier to create a successful social media listening strategy.

Q: What are some of the best social media listening practices that businesses are using with success?

The most authentic sentiment, messaging, and thought around your product happens on social where your consumers are. They don't have an agenda on social, they are just enjoying your product with friends and sharing their experiences. Tapping into those moments and experiences and understanding what experiences inspire people to post on social in the first place is valuable. There is no other source that is more direct when it comes to influencing your product strategy. **–Sirous Wadia, GumGum**

Q: What are some great tools that businesses can use to track social listening?

We use tools such as Sprinklr to see who is saying what and to learn more about the market trends on social. I use a tool called Traackr to track the influencers in my influencer marketing program. We look at Social Mention to see what is happening in the market–from the strength of our brand to the sentiment that is out there as well as our brand vs. competitors. There is another free tool called Mention. It takes the place of Google Alerts, but it has more features. **– Amisha Gandhi, SAP**

One of the tools that I love is called NUVI, which does a lot of influencer identification. It's pretty comprehensive and has Facebook data available. A new tool that has come out is through Reddit. You go to www.reddit.com/domain/yourwebaddress and put your web address there. Then, Reddit will tell you how many articles from your website or from your blog, from that domain, have been submitted to Reddit. It's a good way to listen and see where your information is being seeded into Reddit. **–Serena Ehrlich, Business Wire**

Q: What kinds of trends do you see happening in the social media listening space?

We generally know how people come to our business and how to get them to buy. We have the general overview of that, but we have to get much more granular. In marketing, we just don't have the tools yet and so right now we are writing one message for everybody. One tweet goes to your entire audience for example, but Facebook has messaging tools that include audience optimization tools where literally you can hit your own fan page with highly customizable messaging. No one is doing that and everyone should be using the free audience not paid advertising. It's because of the amount of time that it takes, but that is where I see the future going. **–Serena Ehrlich, Business Wire**

Q: How do you develop a social media listening plan?

It's a matter of understanding what your specific goals are because social media listening can be an unruly mess. There are so many use cases where it can easily become this overwhelming amount of content. You have to know what you need. **–Sirous Wadia, GumGum**

When people get super famous, they get these existing fans that just auto-retweet and they are just people who promote. They are not as engaged. If you get the rising influencers, these people are in it together. Everybody connected to them is in it. Rising influencers are some of the best influencers to work with because their audiences are more engaged. **–Serena Ehrlich, Business Wire**

Social media listening tools from this session:
Sprinklr Sprinklr.com
Traackr Traakr.com
Social Mention SocialMention.com
Mention Mention.com/en
Google Alerts Google.com/alerts
NUVI NUVI.com
Reddit Reddit.com
GumGum gumgum.com/image-recognition/visual-intelligence/

Sports and Social Media Listening

Find out how you can make your brand part of the game-day experience on social.

Here are some key takeaways from this topic:

- **Communicate with–not at–the fans**
  Follow their lead and speak their language, whether it's adopting a popular rallying cry or simply commenting on their Instagram posts.
- **Find fun ways to engage**
  Post polls on social media, or post a photo and invite people to caption it.
  Gauge your social media success
  Measure the response to your tweets and posts and whether or not it's driving traffic to your site.

> **Watch these videos on our website:** Get these session videos delivered to your inbox by registering this book at MediaLeaders.com/dmt/videos/ (and be the first to hear about our next events).

Q: How do you define social media listening? What does it mean to you?

It's all about trying to tap into where the conversations are happening and figuring out where as an individual you need to focus and create the strongest presence. **–David Waterman, The Search Agency**

Social media listening is trying to figure out what content our audience wants to see. Do they want the fun stuff, the serious stuff, the post-game stuff, the fan catching the foul ball with his beer without dropping his kid? We have to listen to what people are saying to figure out what they want. **–Pete Stella, FOX Sports**

Q: How do you interact with your followers and your fans on these platforms?

The polls are really fun. You can put polls on Twitter and Facebook now. I also troll for memes to help find related content and get in on the conversation. Also, in-game tweeting has gotten me so many followers because there are fans who watch Twitter throughout the entire game. **– Shereen Lavi, Rayan Enterprises**

We did a lot of live Q&A's on Facebook when we were at spring training. That seemed to click really well with our fans. Also, something as simple as posting a really great action shot photo on Instagram or Facebook and saying "Caption This" can really bring in engagement. It's surprising how much reach you can get with one photo. **–Pete Stella, FOX Sports**

Fans want to know they are being listened to, even if it's something as simple as liking a tweet or commenting on their Instagram post. **–Neil Horowitz, Hopscotch**

It's about putting content up and taking content down and knowing when to do that. We had an airline client once and any time there was a crash, they pulled any kind of paid social ads to be conscious that after a crash it was not a good idea to ask people to purchase flight tickets. Be sensitive to the actual topic creation that is happening on your social media accounts. **–David Waterman, The Search Agency**

When I was with the Arizona Coyotes, a small hockey team, I noticed that when the team was down or when they were up, this small group of superfans would start howling like coyotes. A couple of them started using this hashtag #rallyhowl, and so I picked up on that. Anytime there was a moment that we wanted the fans back in, we would put that out there: "It's time for a #rallyhowl." By the end of the season, the howling was so loud and it still continues today as a tradition that the fans embrace. So find out what your community is passionate about and figure out how you can seize that, amplify it, and grow it. **–Neil Horowitz, Hopscotch**

Q: How do we know when social media listening is working?

It's about people engaging with your tweets and your posts, but also seeing that it is driving traffic. So, we look at time on site, how many pages are viewed, and how many people are placing links back to your site. **–David Waterman, The Search Agency**

Q: What is so powerful about the superfans that have developed in sports PR? What do you do to leverage this?

There are information systems in sports that can help fans enjoy the sport better from a score bug up in the corner to the way that information is being put on screen or on tools behind-the-scenes. For me, it has to be intuitive. It is all about the designing the experience for the fan and making sure that the information is there when the fans need it, creating the right orchestrated moments. **–Gil Hasam, Troika**

I think sports fans are uniquely capable of expressing their identity that is regional, local, and geographic in nature. It is often tied to family and life experience, who you see as your people. I think sports fans are particularly effective at that expression and communication and reinforcement of personal identity, which is also really critical as a human being. **–Susan Kresnicka, Troika**

VR & AR Technology & Examples

Here are some key takeaways from this topic:

- **Determine the story you are trying to tell**
  Whether you are creating an AR or VR experience, focus
  on telling a story through an overarching experience.
  Consider your customer's journey on how you can use
  AR or VR to improve their experience with your brand.
- **VR is immersive while AR introduces a digital plane
  into real environments**
  A perfect example of AR technology is Pokémon Go,
  which adds a digital plane to the user's real environment.
  VR includes a headset that totally immerses the user into
  that experience.

Watch these videos on our website: Get these session
videos delivered to your inbox by registering this book
at MediaLeaders.com/dmt/videos/ (and be the first to
hear about our next events).

Q: What are some of the things that you are looking for in order to run a successful project using VR & AR technology? What are some of the things that you see that are missing from the table that some of your clients may not always understand?

I think from a creative side it is really determining what is that story that we are telling them and what is the overarching experience. From a retail lens, it is what is the customer's journey and at what point in the customer's journey are we touching them? When are, we telling that story and how are we capturing their attention emotionally? When it relates to VR/AR, it's within the customer journey's path, we need to know at what point do they use the technology to augment the choices that they are making and how do we better their choices and give them the amount of information that they need to make the correct choice for themselves. **–Bryan Pieper, KNOCK**

For us, we have what we think is a very beautiful campus at Chapman University and we have created a virtual tour with VR/AR technology. We love to focus on international recruiting and for those people, if they cannot come to tour the campus and see it, we can give these people the opportunity to tour the campus virtually through a headset or through a 360 video on Facebook. **–David May, Chapman University**

Q: What is the difference between VR and AR?

AR is the introduction of a digital plane into the real environment whereas VR is the introduction of the environment in a digital plane. So, it's a reverse of it. When you have a headset on with VR, you are completely in that environment whereas in AR you have the real world and you are layering on top of that. I think the best example of AR is Pokémon Go. When that became huge, it had an augmented reality component to it that was fairly simple. It put little monsters in the world in front of you using your phone as a viewfinder. We love to build that kind of creative, immersive environment in VR where you are taking yourself out of the world. **–Bryan Pieper, KNOCK**

Q: What is the difference between worlds and realities? How does virtual reality intersect with online virtual games?

I create worlds and not realities. When you go back twenty years, you see the movies like Tron where they depict these online worlds, which were the first form of a virtual reality. You saw this with online RPGs such as EverQuest and World of Warcraft. Those massive multi-player games had people actually living inside of the online world. On the other hand, there were a couple of worlds such as Second Life and Entropia Universe and these were less gamified, but more focused on the true value of your avatar as a reflection of you. Today the Oculus and the Hololens are the virtual reality systems that most people are familiar with. Try to reach people and get them to think about the value of their time. All digital gaming has been so immersive that people have blown hundreds and millions of hours around the world unproductively. It's great fun and developers develop more and more immersive games that are literally designed to take as much of your life as possible. From a marketing perspective, I try to reach people and actually make them think about what they get out of their time inside virtual reality. **–Jon Jacobs, Virtual Reality**

Q: What are some examples of companies using AR/VR technologies?

One example that I have is the Tesla factory and showroom. They use AR/VR technologies to explain to their potential buyers what is going on under the hood. Both of these technologies allow you to take something complex and to allow you to understand it better. If you are already a fan of a product, then being able to understand it at a deeper level gives you that emotional attachment to it and may allow you to sell more. With the technology, you also have a chance to de-mystify things. **–Brandon Middleton, Microsoft**

Q: How do you capture data points related to VR and AR technologies?

You have to build applications, which sit on VR or AR and the way that you build those applications is monitoring what the user is doing whether that is how they are moving their head or -- if you have built a virtual world -- what pieces they are interacting with the most. In terms of how to collect data, you need to work backwards from what your desired outcome is. You need to figure out what data is important to you. **–Brandon Middleton, Microsoft**

Virtual Reality Best Practices

Here are some key takeaways from this topic:

- **Virtual reality makes you feel as if you are actually in the experience**
  It works through the power of sight, which convinces people what they see is real.
- **Find fun ways to engage**
  Post polls on social media, or post a photo and invite people to caption it.
- **The quality of VR applications you invest in should depend on your goals and expectations**
  Everyone has access to YouTube 360 and Facebook 360, which means more people will be exposed to the experience you've created. Tools like Oculus and Vive are on the high end of the VR spectrum, and they're worth the investment for things like special events.
- **No matter how exciting the technology, content remains important**
  Always test market the experience you've created before you launch it. Make improvements if you're not getting the response you want.

Q: How does virtual reality work? What are some examples you have seen where virtual reality is highly effective?

Presence is a key part of VR. There is a sense that you are actually there because your eyes are so powerful. Our power of sight convinces us that if we are seeing something, it is real. Another key component with VR is that when we see something on the screen or read a book, it is a second-order experience. It's something we're watching rather than experiencing. VR is a first-order experience. It affects you as if you are there. For example, they are using it a lot to treat PTSD because they can put people back into a traumatic experience and help them work through. That's a great example that highlights how powerful this technology really is. **–Jodi Schiller, New Reality Arts**

The ability to do dramatic things in VR is a wonderful example of the way VR works. I created an experience with Guillermo del Toro for *Pacific Rim* where you get to be a Jaeger pilot in one of the giant robots. You feel like you are there, and it is a super cool experience. We also did a piece for GE for their factory tour, and it wasn't exciting to me at first, but the VR element takes the tour from boring to captivating. Immediately, you become engaged. **–Dale Carman, Groove Jones**

Q: What is the best way to get started with practical applications for brands and companies?

The one that I always show people for the first time is Tilt Brush because the learning curve is pretty short and intuitive. They stand still and then create and draw. The creative element is so strong in this game. Any time that you can get people to be creative with your brand it will increase the replay value of the experience, and they want to share the experience with their friends. **–Ned Atkins, UploadVR**

On the low end of the VR spectrum, you have YouTube 360 and Facebook 360, which you can view on any phone and everybody can participate now with that. The next step up is Google Cardboard and then Samsung Gear followed by the Oculus and then Vive. For brand activation, a lot of times we will have brands that want to avoid using Vive because they want more people to be able to access to their VR tool. Our strategy is that if the client is going to have an event, we will use the Vive because the opportunity to really impact people is incredible. If not, we will go with one of the more accessible VR tools. **–Dale Carman, Groove Jones**

If you are trying VR for the first time, there is the technology and then there is the experience. They are not mutually exclusive. As the technology gets better and better, the cost goes up. If you are looking to explore VR for the first time, be aware that you could have a less-than-stellar technology experience because the viewer may be low end on the phone, but it could still be a quality experience. The story that the experience is telling is really important. **–Robin Kim, Ruder Finn**

Q: What are some "Do's and Don'ts" for VR? How do people get started in actually creating VR content?

My favorite VR experiences have three elements: the creative freedom element where can create something new and novel every time, the social element where you can interact with others in VR, and the storytelling element where the VR experience includes a great interactive story. As far as creating VR content, UploadVR is starting a VR code academy to help developers learn VR code and make it easier for brands and companies to hire people who can create VR content for them. **–Ned Atkins, UploadVR**

The biggest failure point that I have seen is that people are so in love with the technology and so in love with the first-time response, they actually forget about the experience. If you have created something and are getting ready to put it out into the world, get people to try it first–preferably people who have seen different kinds of VR before. **–Robin Kim, Ruder Finn**

Live Video: YouTube Live vs Facebook Live

Here are some key takeaways from this panel:

- **People are influenced by other people**
  People are interested in learning trends and topics from people they are interested in. Consider creating your live videos with an influencer, this can expand your social reach as increase engagement.
- **Both platforms have pros and cons**
  Facebook Live generally has better video quality, but Facebook makes it difficult to share that video on other platforms once the broadcast is finished. YouTube offers better monetization and archival opportunities.
- **Audio is important**
  Live videos, especially event-driven live videos, should have clear audio. Without clear audio, you may risk having an unusable video.

Watch these videos on our website: Get these session videos delivered to your inbox by registering this book at MediaLeaders.com/dmt/videos/ (and be the first to hear about our next events).

Q: What are some of the best practices and innovative strategies of digital live video?

When you think about the audience that you want to reach, how do you reach them? We can always put a great spokesperson or a customer with a spokesperson and talk about a product or a brand, which could be interesting but influencers take things to another level. People are interested in trends and topics and are influenced by people that they are interested in or would like to get advice from. This is what an influencer can be. We work with influencers to co-create content or to publish content that they are creating around an interesting trend or topic. **–Amisha Gandhi, SAP**

We launched the first ever "live film festival" on Facebook and reached out to different motor-themed filmmakers who made short films anywhere from 10 to 45 minutes in length. We did a deal with them that would allow us to stream their films live on Facebook so it became more like a traditional broadcast platform, but we had the filmmakers interacting with fans in the comments "live". It was pre-planned, event programming so everyone knows that 11AM it's Biker Movie Sunday (TM) and we promote that across all of our channels, through our newsletters, on our social, everywhere. We used Wirecast to stream through the Facebook API. **–Zack Coffman, One World Studios Ltd.**

When we talk about all different types of content marketing and inbound marketing, we know that there are multiple platforms that can do a lot of different things and streaming video is no different. It's a matter of knowing your audience and what the demographics are of the people that you are trying to reach. Where are the people you want to interact with? **–David May, Chapman University**

Q: Is there a winner or a clear leader in the field at the moment between YouTube Live and Facebook Live?

For us, we use both but we have used Facebook Live more because the video quality is much higher and so when we take a look at these live videos when we are done, we can put them in other social media channels as well. YouTube compresses so we lost some of the quality and couldn't reuse the footage. Facebook also has set up the algorithms so that when you use Facebook Live, it shows up in all of your follower's feeds more. It gives you that bump, but YouTube also has a built-in audience and it is easy to share outside of the YouTube platform. Those are some of the pros and cons for us. **–Amisha Gandhi, SAP**

I think Facebook Live is the winner because the two things you need are an audience and great content. Facebook already has the audience and now people are going there to create great content. Building a huge audience, especially in live, is almost impossible for anyone else to do. As you compare Facebook Live to YouTube, which has had a live product for a long time, you don't see the same success. The way that people engage on YouTube is much more search driven or driven by a particular creator who they love and who they want to engage with. It's not driven as much by let me browse around and see who is live. However, we are hearing from creators that YouTube is a better place to store your library of content. Facebook has made it hard to film a video on Facebook Live and then publish it on to YouTube as well. Some creators are actually thinking about, "Do we double record our live presentation into both platforms?" mainly because they are thinking about how to have that archival footage live in a place where they can have a monetization opportunity, which is available on YouTube and not on Facebook at the moment. **–Brian Nickerson, MagicLinks**

Q: What advice would you give to anyone either embarking in live video or developing a platform or content in live video?

Any time there is an early stage on a new platform, there is an opportunity for first mover advantage. My number one piece of advice to a creator would be to pick up platforms and embrace them, go for it from the start. If you take Instagram for example and the launch of their new short stories. In Instagram, if you are doing those stories and doing video, then the algorithms are going to start taking over and you are going to show up more for your friends and people who are not your friends yet but might be interested in your content. From an influencer perspective, embrace it and be early. **–Brian Nickerson, MagicLinks**

There are a lot of resources online where you can sort of raise your level of professionalism of your hosts or yourself (if you are the host). It's pretty standard stuff, but if you can learn a few tricks it can really engage. One trick we did, was give a "giveaway" whenever things started to get a little quiet on the live platform we were on. It kept people interested and intrigued and it helped us grow our audience. **–Zack Coffman, One World Studios Ltd.**

Audience Q: How do you incorporate live stream videos into events that are already happening? What are the basic needs that you need in order to live stream?

I think audio is really important especially when you are at an event. We learned the hard way, where we didn't have the plug-in mic to the iPhone and things like that so we actually ran out and got the plug-ins and put it into the microphone and even though it was so noisy, we got clear audio. There are lots of different attachments that you can get for iPad, iPhone, Android devices, etc. Without a quality sound, your video is really unusable. **–Amisha Gandhi, SAP**

Ask the stakeholders who are asking for that experience with a live event about the kind of experience they want. This is one of those things where you can spend nothing and you can spend a ton of money, and you get what you pay for. If you are unwilling to put in the time or the money, the quality will be lower. **–David May, Chapman University**

YouTube vs. Facebook Video

Here are some key takeaways from this panel:

- **Consider your end goal for posting video**
  In many cases you can make good money posting a video on YouTube–but if you're looking to build your audience, Facebook is often the better choice.
- **Live streaming can be exciting, but consider the content**
  If the content is fast paced and the audience wants it right then, great. If not, it might make more sense to spend time editing and posting it for greater longevity.
- **The video's length should dictate where it goes**
  People seek out and expect longer videos on YouTube, but almost no one will watch more than a minute or two on Facebook.

Watch these videos on our website: Get these session videos delivered to your inbox by registering this book at MediaLeaders.com/dmt/videos/ (and be the first to hear about our next events).

Q: YouTube and Facebook have both been around for a long time, but the video portion of Facebook is really heating up. What are you noticing in that space? What is on the top of your mind when it comes to YouTube and Facebook?

It's very interesting. I think what is pertinent is the reasoning behind why you would use one platform vs. the other. The reasons that YouTube is successful are still there, but it is interesting to see the way Facebook is allowing you to quickly capture something and engage with somebody at that moment. **–Jacquelle Amankonah, Google**

I think the really exciting trend right now is live streaming. Facebook Live was available to brands, pages, and celebrities for a long time, but it is now available to everybody. The walls have come down, people do not expect it to be produced, and it is creating an authenticity to where you don't have to be intimidated or know anything technical. As long as you have a phone, you can be live. And Google has an option with Hangouts on Air. **–Virginia Nussey, Bruce Clay, Inc.**

The difference between Facebook and YouTube is a push vs. a pull. Facebook is based on a social platform, where YouTube is a video player platform. For YouTube, you search for your videos to play. On Facebook, they are presented to you from your friends. I think where Facebook has the social, YouTube has the search. **–Chadwick Sahleye, Social Bluebook**

Most creators think of their presence as not being YouTube specific, Facebook specific or Snapchat specific, etc. They think about how to present their personal brand across whatever medium is available to them. They will often take a project and distribute it in various ways across these platforms. You have all of these different methods of interacting through video, all driving high engagement but accomplishing different things for the creator's brands. – **Ben Williams, Reelio, Inc.**

Q: Tell me about the different mindsets of the audiences. What is the difference between a YouTube audience and a Facebook audience?

The mindset is the key differentiation point between Facebook and YouTube. People are thinking with YouTube that they are intentionally going to look for content. It's where they go for information just like they do with the Google search bar. This is where you can choose how you want to represent your brand. For Facebook, it is more, "I'm scrolling and seeing what my friends are recommending to me," and so it is about on-the-go and capturing something that you are doing. **–Jacquelle Amankonah, Google**

Could you ever imagine someone uploading a video to YouTube without sound and trying to hook someone in? It would never work. Yet on Facebook, this has become a strategy to add subtitles and almost create a silent movie on Facebook. **–Rich DeMuro, KTLA-TV**

How many of you follow Tasty on Facebook? They manage to capture your attention because your friends have shared that content and their content goes viral. It is really well done and made for Facebook, so it doesn't have to have sound–but you have to think how you will grab people's attention. It could be through text or with some fast cuts. You also have to think about how many people are going to watch the complete video. On YouTube, people will watch a 10 to 15-minute video, because they go into it knowing that's what it is. On Facebook, no one will sit through a 10-minute video because most people are on their phones and scrolling through their feeds. **–Adam Gausepohl, PopShorts**

Q: Speaking of views, Facebook reports a view after three seconds and YouTube reports a view after 30 seconds. How does that play into things?

It very much goes to the question of the content. When you are thinking about how to measure a view, the views are not worth the same amount, because on YouTube content it is usually a much more in-depth, engaged view. On Facebook, a view will get 80% of its view in the first 24 hours, where on YouTube it will be more like 30%. When you think about someone who subscribes to a channel and watches every video that a creator puts out, they can consume more of the branded content in a more organic way. **–Ben Williams, Reelio, Inc.**

Right now, a lot of people are jumping over to Facebook to try to get that traffic but they aren't making any money on Facebook, at least not through Facebook directly. I think whichever one of these platforms ends up helping the creators make the most money, they are going to win this race. **–Chadwick Sahleye, Social Bluebook**

It came out recently that you have to tag a brand. Facebook's rules with brand sponsorship was a little iffy for a while, but they clarified that you now have to tag the brand. I think adding a little bit of paid advertising can go a long way as well. **–Adam Gausepohl, PopShorts**

Q: Virginia, you said you like what The White House and "The Today Show" are doing with Facebook Live. Why is that?

They are big names, but you can take a lot of examples out of the kinds of things that Facebook Live offers. I would emphasize that the rawness and the ability to be creative without worrying about a certain production quality level is exciting. Of course, your goals should also come first. If you are looking for money, it's YouTube, and if you are looking to build your audience, it's Facebook. **–Virginia Nussey, Bruce Clay, Inc.**

I knew somebody who made $20,000 on a YouTube video post. They stuck the same video up on Facebook and got four times the viewership, but they made nothing there. **– Chadwick Sahleye, Social Bluebook**

I am not really sold on this Live thing, to be honest. I don't watch Periscope ever because I don't care about watching someone live. If I am watching Tasty on Facebook, it is interesting because it so cut up and edited, and that is how I want to watch something. You have to get my attention quickly. If they were just there cooking live, I would get bored and leave. I think you can only do live if is genuinely interesting live. I'm interested to see where it goes, but I'm not fully sold. **–Adam Gausepohl, PopShorts**

When it is done being live, it is literally almost worthless. There is almost a reason to not watch when you see it was live. You scroll through and you see that it was live and say, "I'm not going to watch it now–I missed it." **–Rich DeMuro, KTLA-TV**

Q: Facebook puts in video with a high-engagement priority, and when you are live, they push that up to the top of the feed because they want to get people in there. So, let's talk about this Wendy's ad.

The Wendy's ad was a case study that was done where the same video was placed on YouTube and Facebook. With the Facebook version of it, they garnered 80% of the views within the first 24 hours and then it trailed off pretty quickly. It stopped receiving reasonable-sized views after 48 or 50 hours. The YouTube version of it garnered a lot less in the first 24 hours, something along the lines of half of the overall views when compared to Facebook, but it continued garnering views for another two to three weeks. The overall view count and overall engagement were far higher for much longer on YouTube. This does seem to suggest that Facebook is very high for a shorter period of time, while YouTube is something that lives there...truly evergreen content. People are used to interacting with YouTube in an evergreen sense. **–Ben Williams, Reelio, Inc.**

Q: What new tools are you using?

I think the most exciting thing is not even the video format itself but some of the ways that people have begun to build the ecosystem around it. One of the slyest moves that

YouTube did and Google at large was Google Cardboard–
the $20 viewer that is not true VR but it gives you a better
experience for doing 360 or surround video. It is a
surprisingly better experience through that simple interface
and gives people a taste for what VR could be. The new gear
is also pretty interesting, the GoPro and new Samsung gear.
Hardware stuff goes along with the software stuff in helping
to transform the way that creators are able to make this new
kind of content such as LiveStream concerts. **–Ben Williams,
Reelio, Inc.**

Part 2: Influence

Influencer campaigns focus on leveraging digital leaders to share your brand message and authentically engage with a larger audience. Typically, brands will connect with an influencer who aligns with their target market to create social posts and/or content marketing, in the voice of the influencer. Brands are utilizing influencer campaigns to natively reach their audience, where they already are, and engage with them.

Is your brand Light, Bright and Polite online?

Our team works with brands of all sizes to ensure their brand message is Light, Bright and Polite.

Get a digital brand audit from our team to see how your customers are finding you (and what they think about your online footprint).

Visit MediaLeaders.com/Audit

Our online audit includes:
10 page customized report with your brand's online footprint
- We show you positive mentions that can be utilized for content marketing
- We highlight negative results and give you multiple suggestions on how to remove them
- We provide a custom video library designed to help your brand to improve its online footprint
- Also learn:
    - How content marketing can build a pipeline of prospects
    - Influencer marketing tips
    - Social media tips for reputation management
    - 5 key tips your brand can use to improve your online presence

Visit MediaLeaders.com/Audit to learn more

Influencer Marketing Tools & Campaign Tips

Here are some key takeaways from this topic:

- **Influencer marketing doesn't need to be complex**
Influencer marketing is interacting and engaging bloggers and influencers. You don't need software, expensive tools or a huge network in order to be successful with influencer marketing.
- **Trust influencers to build brand perception**
Brands who develop authentic influencer relationships tend to boost community development and brand perception. Audiences respond to brand messaging when it doesn't always come from the brand.
- **Think about how your brand can help influencers**
If you start your influencer campaign trying to determine what influencers can do for you then you will not get the best results. Consider how you can help influencers, like helping them build their audience or increase awareness in your industry.

Q: How would you define influencer marketing?

I think with influencer marketing, everybody thinks that you need software, you need lots of connections with influencers and celebrities, and I don't think that's true at all. I got started in influencer marketing because I had an e-commerce site and we would simply email bloggers cold, ask them if they wanted to review our product for free, and without spending anything we got over $100,000 in sales from those bloggers. I would define influencer marketing as interacting and engaging with bloggers and influencers. It doesn't need to be any more complex than that. **–Jesse Leimgruber, NeoReach**

Influencer marketing is both a marketing channel (a way to reach your customers in an authentic way) and it's also a brand building initiative (the ability to enhance your brand through the different brands and audiences of different influencers). **–Andrew Higgins, Pixlee**

Q: How is influencer marketing changing?

I think we are in a transitional phase right now, especially for consumer brands where we are getting a little over saturated and our audience is starting to be able to figure out that there isn't real intent or affinity behind a lot of influencer marketing. So, what brands are really starting to do is the community development and that is because brand perception is not really controlled by the brand anymore. Influencer marketing is transitioning into, "How do I really build relationships and where is the best place to start?" **–Andrew Higgins, Pixlee**

Q: How can you develop influencer relationships?

Start with a handshake and end with a hug. Maintain your influencer relationships by having conversations with them and sending them cool products from time to time. **–Pegah Kamal, Aruba, a Hewlett Packard Enterprise company**

If you start thinking, "What can the influencer do for me?" then you have already lost that battle. It's too late. You've lost it. It's too late. It doesn't matter how you approach the campaign, your results will be disappointing. **–Pierre Loic Assayag, Traackr**

It's all about relationships. If you are not being authentic, things will not work. That being said, I would be lying if I would say we didn't see campaigns that saw ridiculously high ROIs, from $20,000 of investment yielding $1m+ in sales, that were fairly inauthentic. I don't think these will last forever and I think they are a short run game, but there are some tactical ways that you can create these types of campaigns. With this particular example, there was one thing that the brand did differently from a tactical perspective that made all the difference. They found bloggers that were really already advocates of the brand's product by looking at their existing followers, but the tactic they used was asking these bloggers to write a review on their product vs. one of their competitors. This allowed the brand to siphon off a lot of the competitor's traffic and it worked really well for them. **–Jesse Leimgruber, NeoReach**

One of the first questions I always ask influencers that I want to connect with is, "How do you like to engage with brands?" Then I ask, "What is it that I can offer you - is it access to our large ecosystem or awareness for yourself in the space?" Then we work together in our programs to help them get what they need and we get what we want. **– Amisha Gandhi, SAP**

Q: What are some tools that you use in the influencer marketing space?

Traackr has a free online course that is really informative so I would recommend going there first because it does so much explaining about what it is, how you divide up your audience, and how to get ROI. **–Pegah Kamal, Aruba, a Hewlett Packard Enterprise company**

I would start with social listening because you understand your own brand and your own customer, but you have to figure out if you have adjacent topics, interests, and concepts that would be relevant to your audience and then find those influencers. Crimson Hexagon, Sprinklr, Hootsuite, Mention, and Google Trends are all great tools that you can use. **–Andrew Higgins, Pixlee**

Social Mention will also help you learn about the strength of your brand and where you stand in the marketplace. **– Amisha Gandhi, SAP**

Influencer Campaign Best Practices

Here are some key takeaways from this panel:

- **Allow influencers to speak in their own voice**
  Don't try to use an influencer as a paid spokesperson who's going to read from a script. Remember that they built their audience based on their unique style, and that audience will tune out if the message or style seems forced or dictated.
- **Consider using small–and mid-sized influencers if it's a good fit**
  Their audience base might be smaller but ultimately more loyal to that influencer–and therefore more receptive to your message.
- **Research the influencers you want to work with**
  AI tools like CharlieApp.com and CrystalKnows.com will give you information about the influencers before you meet them and even offer suggestions on how to better connect.
- **It's okay to let on that this is sponsored content**
  If an influencer is excited about being associated with your brand–which is what you want, anyway–there's no reason to hide that they're also being paid to help promote it. Audiences respect transparency

Q: What are the best practices that you are seeing in influencer marketing for brands?

Understand what influencer marketing is. What it is **not** is a paid commercial. This has gone down over the past year, but a lot of the brands that we worked with in the past were basically viewing these influencers as actors in commercials delivering talking points in the brand's voice, and according to the brand's style. That is not influencer marketing. Influencer marketing is using that influencer's audience and who the audience knows that influencer to be, to engage with them in an authentic way. **–Adam Hendle, FameBit**

For brands, it is really important to understand the target market. Be really clear about who those influencers are that you are interested in and what level of influencer you are interested in. **–Laurel Mintz, Elevate My Brand**

I think the most important thing is to really understand your influencer, get to know them and what their personal brand is, what they represent as an influencer and how you use what their brand is to benefit you. You build a relationship with an influencer and take everything that is making them successful and transition that back into your brand. That is the way that you build a meaningful piece of content that is going to feel organic and not like an ad. The last thing you want is to make a video and have the top comment be "sellout." **–Jay Boice, NeoReach**

Sometimes the best value comes from using a niche blogger. On Twitter, we've found that we have great penetration with sneakerheads. One of our influencers tweeted a single tweet about the new Nike Lady Liberty sneakers that had just been released. It generated about $300,000 in sales and $30,000 in commission revenue. Obviously, that is an outlier, but it is by no means exceptional. This influencer had a community of highly engaged sneakerhead fans. We see good micro verticals with that when there is a strong, highly engaged community. **–Oliver Roup, VigLink**

Q: So, a big thing we've heard so far is not to try and use influencers as advertising. For brands who are then thinking about their message and how to get it out there, what do you think influencer marketing best solves for them?

Getting connected to their core audience. More and more now that we know that digital is the future and mobile is now, and that you have to reach your audience where they are. One of the best things influencers can do for a brand is really raise the bar and create great content exactly where their end user is. **–Laurel Mintz, Elevate My Brand**

A lot of brands have a challenging time producing content because it can be time intensive and resource heavy, and you might not have a videographer on staff. Leveraging influencers is a way to generate content that you know is going to be engaging and authentic and perfect for these social channels. **–Sae Cho, Horizon Media**

Q: What are your favorite tools and how do you use them?

CharlieApp.com, CrystalKnows.com, and Nova. These are AI tools that I use personally when I am trying to engage with people that I think will have influence for the brand that I am representing at any given point in time. Charlie essentially extracts information from publicly available websites and sends you an email with a summary of the person that you are about to engage with. So, it's a very interesting way of scrapping information. You can use it on a personal level when you are getting ready for a meeting, but when you are reaching out to somebody that is key because you have to know who is in front of you. My favorite, because it is the creepiest, is CrystalKnows. It is fascinating. It breaks down the best ways to engage with people in meetings and via email. **–Jock Breitwieser, TriNet**

Q: There are all of these different levels of influencers. We have meta-influencers who are social celebrities in their own right, and then we have micro-influencers who may have fewer than 10,000 followers but an incredibly engaged audience. How do you guys leverage all those different levels of influence?

There is a lot of value being overlooked in these small and mid-size influencers. When I say small, I am talking about 5,000 subscribers on YouTube up to 250,000. There is a lot of really good value because those people have very tight engagement with their audience. They are like friends. When you get over a certain mark, you are not a friend anymore–you are a celebrity, and that relationship is a little bit different. When you are friends with somebody, the trust is higher. It can be easier for a friend to sell your product than a celebrity. **–Adam Hendle, FameBit**

And the reverse as well. When you do have someone with 500,000 YouTube followers and they endorse a product, it gives that product a level of credibility that you can't get out of the smaller influencer. That also creates share ability, which might end up putting CutiePie's video on Reddit. That also lends that brand credibility to see it across other shared platforms. **–Jay Boice, NeoReach**

I think the smaller influencers try harder. They are still building their brand, so they think that you are bringing as much value to them as they are to you, and it can be a more mutually beneficial relationship. **–Laurel Mintz, Elevate My Brand**

Q: What do you guys think about the future for bloggers and influencers going multi-channel?

It is very important that influencers can transition from one platform to multi-platform because it allows multiple channels to acquire users and go where the best ROI is at the time. That's better for brands as well. Blogging has become a gateway to vlogging, and vlogging has become one of the most influential ways to do influencer marketing because it is directly speaking about the brand in everyday life to people and fans. **–Jay Boice, NeoReach**

Live-streaming platforms are very interesting, especially on Periscope and now Facebook. It is the rawest way that influencers can interact with their audience. Facebook is exponentially growing, and influencers are going back to it. **–Adam Hendle, FameBit**

Q: Speaking of live stream, do you guys have any best practices for brands? It can be pretty scary for a brand to say "Stream yourself live" because there is no opportunity to preview content or know what is going to

come out of someone's mouth. Is there any way for a brand to prepare the influencer without stepping on creativity?

It comes down to making sure that the live stream isn't your first platform with that influencer. Make sure you have a relationship with that influencer, that you have done other things and had success. If they have shown that they understand your brand, then you can feel more at ease with allowing an influencer to live stream. **–Adam Hendle, FameBit**

We always develop cross-marketing documents for influencers and the brands so that we all know best practices as well as do's and don'ts, so we are clear. We also do audits of the influencers from time to time to make sure that they really understand the brand. **–Laurel Mintz, Elevate My Brand**

Do a kick-off call. Don't be afraid to ask to get the campaign manager, the influencer, and yourself on a call to make sure that everybody is on the same page. Everybody knows what needs to happen. Most influencers are not going to be opposed to that whatsoever–they want to know, too. **–Jay Boice, NeoReach**

I would try to capture live content, but really keep in mind what you are doing to create a more curated story that you can edit together so you really get the best of both worlds. **– Peyton Dougherty, PopShorts**

Q: How do we measure influencer campaigns in terms of KPI?

Engagement. It's just like any great social platform–you can have an influencer with a million followers, but if those followers are not talking and engaging with a campaign, the brand or the influencer themselves, then it is a totally worthless campaign in my mind. Engagement is more important than numbers. **–Laurel Mintz, Elevate My Brand**

The sources of traffic are key. In the influencer world, it is not necessarily the major celebrities that you have to pay big bucks for driving all the conversions. The value really comes from that mid-tier influencer with a fan base of real people actually reading their stuff and engaging. So, Google Analytics allows you to really understand where the traffic comes from. **–Oliver Roup, VigLink**

Always incorporate something that's trackable so that you can also monetize it and it can help to pay back your influencers. **–Josh Ochs, Media Leaders**

We do a lot of live events, and so when we do an influencer campaign, there is a direct ROI there. We are able to measure that in a way that is inclusive of the online impressions and engagements, so for us, there is a real return that our clients can see on the day of the event. **–Laurel Mintz, Elevate My Brand**

Outside of tracking links and descriptions, we have also seen coupon codes work really well. A lot of times viewers watch the piece of content and think it's cool, so they go open up another tab and Google that. But the coupon code incentivizes them to take action, and then that is also trackable. So, make sure for every influencer you have a different coupon code so you can see who is driving the most sales. **–Adam Hendle, FameBit**

Encourage user-generated content. Hold contests. Really get people pumped up because some of the things that get our top influencers' fans the most excited is having the opportunity to be featured on an influencer's Twitter feed, for example. **–Peyton Dougherty, PopShorts**

How do I know that I am getting the fair market value? How do I know that this is being priced correctly? Do you guys have a model that you use?

For us, we get handed a chunk of budget and have to determine what that looks like for the influencers. We have to take into account the influencer component and the production needs. We know what our margins need to be and then we peel out the pieces for the influencers accordingly. **–Laurel Mintz, Elevate My Brand**

We come at it from a bit of a different approach because we are an open marketplace. When you launch your campaign, you will receive upwards of 100 different proposals and see what their average views are per video, what their audience looks like, what their price is, and what they are promising me for the campaign. It is really up to you as the brand to weigh options and pick what you think is the best value. **– Adam Hendle, FameBit**

Q: There are people who are obviously creating content that they have received compensation for, but there are few guidelines or enforceable laws about how to disclose that relationship between an influencer and a brand. How do you incorporate that disclosure in a natural way that is not going to be awkward for fans?

The bottom line is that you have to be clear. If you hide it in there, it is just going to come back and bite you. If the influencers have taken it and they are proud of it, you can see it. If the influencers are excited about the sponsorship, there should be no reason to hide it, so it must be positively disclosed in all video and descriptive content. As long as the influencer really believes in the product and the brand, it shouldn't come across as something that is slimy. **–Adam Hendle, FameBit**

It is about transparency. When it is a good fit with an influencer, they are excited about it. When we do brand takeovers, it is obvious–they are on the brand platform and saying who they are and what they are doing. And people know that it is pay-to-play now, so it makes it a lot easier. **– Laurel Mintz, Elevate My Brand**

What would be one or two tools you would recommend for somebody who is just getting their feet wet in influencer marketing?

If you are doing this for the first time, hire an agency or consultant who knows this space really well and can walk you through it at least the first time so that you understand. It will help you ramp up your campaigns that much faster. **– Laurel Mintz, Elevate My Brand**

As far as testing things, I would try to keep it above a super-minimum budget because it is hard to gauge the success of a campaign below a certain threshold. **–Peyton Dougherty, PopShorts**

Media Leaders–the company that hosts this conference– bought an influencer network in 2015. I have a tactical tool we use that helps. When we are looking for bloggers to add to our brand-friendly influencer network, which has about 4,000 influencers now (they are not the neoreach people. NeoReach has people in the millions, and they do an amazing job), but we are focused more on the little campaigns and use a tool called Ninja Outreach. It is free for the first few searches and helps you look at bloggers when you do not have the budget to hire an agency or consultant to help you out. It lets you collect bloggers and influencers that you like and add them to a list–because this is really an organization game at the end of the day in order to find people who fit your brand and its core message now. **–Josh Ochs, Media Leaders**

Q: How can brands woo talent over?

When I was talent, I was really just interested in finding brands that wanted to work with me and would allow me to do what I wanted to do in my voice, in my style. What's really cool are influencer experiences that we have seen brands start to experiment with. For example, sending someone to a movie premiere is a really engaging and enticing way to attract an influencer by using something that they cannot go out and buy on their own. It also creates great content in the process. **–Adam Hendle, FameBit**

So much of it is about building that relationship with the influencer from the beginning. With any sort of outreach, you don't have to be stiff about it. You can be friendly and casual and really try to speak to and understand them as an influencer. They will respond to that much better than sending a business-style email saying, "We want to pay you."
–Jay Boice, NeoReach

The best information we get on influencers comes from other influencers. If there is someone you are working with who you think is doing an awesome job, ask them or see who they are working with, collaborating with, and tagging.
–Peyton Dougherty, PopShorts

Q: Any horror stories?

Influencers cursing on channels. That is a really good one. **– Laurel Mintz, Elevate My Brand**

We had a few times where an influencer will make the video, never get the approval and throw it up on their channel. The brand will freak out and say, "That's not how we wanted this to look," so we have to get them to take it down. That is usually a bad situation. **–Jay Boice, NeoReach**

For us, the problem is that you can have everything arranged, and then on the set day, they will say "I have this other thing..." So, to avoid that, create copy and film ahead. Even on Snapchat. Review editing. There has to be a process. **–Peyton Dougherty, PopShorts**

10 influencer campaign deal killers

A humorous take on what brands don't want

Here are some key takeaways from this panel:

- **Empower your creators.**
  Don't micromanage influencers. Influencers understand their audience better than anyone else so it's important to allow them to create content in their voice. When there is little-to-none brand interference, campaigns inevitably come across as more authentic.
- **Focus on building content specifically for each platform.**
  It would be a mistake to ignore social platforms for influencer campaigns. Determine where your audience spends time and what they like to see on those platforms, then create content based on that data. Consistently examine your insights so you can continue to improve your content.
- **Utilize live video.**
  With platforms like YouTube and Facebook prioritizing live video there is a huge opportunity for brands and influencers to engage their audience, in a new way. Determine a tactical strategy for creating and promoting live video. Then create your videos with a purpose and offer value to your viewers.

Q: What was your biggest influencer marketing fail and what did you learn from it?

A drone manufacturer reached out to a tech influencer we worked with, and wanted this particular influencer to feature a drone in one of their videos, for free. Although they didn't want to pay for it, they did want control over what the video would look like. Finally, the drone manufacturer said "We'll give you 50% of a drone. You can buy it." The newest version of a $1500 drone, the influencer would still have to buy $750. He was not happy about that.

The selling point of the drone was that it has software that tells the drone when there is a tree or something similar and keeps it from crashing. So, the influencer decided to make this video about "how can we crash the drone?" Although the influencer was able to crash the drone, it produced a more authentic video for his audience. He got great engagement on that video, more fans seeing it, and great results for the client. Also, it probably helped him in future videos because it wasn't a story about "why this drone is so great," it was a story about "hey, the main form of marketing for this particular drone is that it can't crash and guess what, I crashed it." **–Brian Nickerson, MagicLinks**

When you are choosing influencers for your campaign, make sure that their audience is similar to the audience that you want to target. So, working for a beauty brand, we were trying to reach girls and women. A lot of influencers on Instagram, such as models, looked like they would attract girls and women, when in reality their audience was mostly men. We have learned to ask influencers who their audience is because they know it best–that is their brand, their job. – **Donna Maher, Marketing Strategy Consultant**

Q: What does "authentic" mean to you and how does it integrate with business?

Authentic to me means not worrying about what other people think, speaking and connecting from the heart. I think when you are being vulnerable it creates a space for people to open up, to share, and to talk. What you see a lot of influencers do is just that. They are opening up their homes, the camera is always on, they are sharing things about their lives that most of us would feel is private, etc. In lots of ways it is important to have that element of authenticity that is real and yeah, sometimes brands or influencers try to fake it, but at the end of the day, people know if you are real or not. **–Donna Maher, Marketing Strategy Consultant**

An influencer has to be true to their own brand first, in order to be authentic, and that is a tough pill for a lot of brands to swallow. Influencers protect their own brand, and they care about a sponsored brand only to the extent that it reflects well on them... So, once you have the initial conversations with the influencer, and do the due diligence, have the respect to get out of their way, and do not micromanage them. **–Ryan Fey, Omelet**

Q: You have seen the change from the more traditional world to the multi-channel world, how is that affecting your work?

We were, as far as I know, the first company to use a social network to sell a movie directly to fans. In 2005, we used Myspace and we sold DVDs of our first movie, and we sold a lot of them. That encouraged us.

This new thing, social marketing, became very comfortable and native to us. Now that we have more channels, it becomes about where does a particular piece of content want to live? We look at the channels as rivers, and we make it an internal policy to never swim against the current. We could cry all day that Facebook changed an algorithm, or what we used to do for SEO on Google Search doesn't work anymore or YouTube or whatever, but at the end of the day you play in their sandbox. If a tactic doesn't work anymore, it doesn't mean that the platform is bad, it means that you just have to figure out what is good. You still have your audience at the end of the day and that is the currency of an influencer or a brand in my opinion. You have to build your audience and the money will come. **–Zack Coffman, One World Studios Ltd.**

When we sit down with influencers, the first thing we ask is "How can we help you? What are you guys doing and can we just listen to what you are doing for a while?" It's great. – **Peter Abraham, Content Marketing & Branding Expert**

Q: What are the best practices that you see right now that are working for you?

The notion of authenticity for a creator is number one. I think finding a place where the brand and the creator really align is critical. One thing that doesn't work is when brands say, "What we want is authenticity, we want to empower people to say what they want to say," and that sounds good but then they don't embody that message. We will show them some creators that can actually do that and their response is, "What is that creator going to say? How can we tell them what to say? Where can we do it?" You see that breakdown in message where the brand has listened to what the buzz words are, but they aren't actually inviting that or empowering creators. **–Brian Nickerson, MagicLinks**

Figure out a strategy and go live tactically. Don't ever do something if you don't know what the point of doing it is. You can still plan, even a live show, because you know that you are about to go live. Take a few minutes and figure out what you are going to do. What is the purpose of doing this live show? Right now, everyone wants live content. YouTube just tweaked their algorithm a few weeks ago, and they are actually giving live video preference. We all know with Facebook Live your followers get a ping every time that you go online. Do your research, look at your insights and find out when most of your people are online and when they are engaging online so you can go live then. Then hang out, stay live, find ways to stretch the show without being lame. **–Zack Coffman, One World Studios Ltd.**

I have used TapInfluence.com as well as Octoly.com. Those are platforms that connect you to influencers and I would definitely recommend them. I think it is a great way to get connected with influencers because you are not sending a contract that could be intimidating, you are negotiating things right there in the platform. I personally prefer just doing old school research on the platform. For example I would look for a YouTube researcher on YouTube, but I have seen that those influencer platforms have been successful as well. **–Donna Maher, Marketing Strategy Consultant**

One tool that I love is Epoxy. They approached the creation of their dashboard in a wonderful way, compared to the big players. You can switch between all of your channels really quickly. Additionally, you can see who commented, and then they order that list for you by the number of followers. It also breaks down your posts to show which posts received the most comments so you can see things instantly. **–Zack Coffman, One World Studios Ltd.**

How Influencer Messages Can Attract the Right Brands

How to determine if a brand is a good fit for your followers

Here are some key takeaways from this panel:

- **Make it easy for brands to reach you**
  For influencers it's important for you to have your contact information readily available for brands. Ensure that you have a contact page on your site, contact information across all of your social platforms, and consider creating a media kit.
- **Don't be afraid to reach out to brands**
  If you're an influencer, who is just starting out, don't be afraid to contact brands directly and ask if you can sample some of their product in exchange for social or blog posts. Most brands are going to be willing to give you something, so that is a great way to start building a brand-influencer relationship.
- **Create compelling content**
  Brands want to work with influencers who have compelling content, whether that's videos, blog posts, or podcasting. If you have a strong point of view, as an influencer, you are going to attract brands within your niche.

Q: If you are an influencer, where do you begin to engage with the brands if you are open to integrating a brand's

message into your audience through your dialogue and your content?

First and foremost, make sure that they can find a way to contact you. Make sure that your website, your Twitter, are up-to-date and you are very clear with people about how they can contact you.

Have a media kit, a "work with me" page or site that says who you want to work with. Be very clear about what you are looking for and what partners you want to work with. As a brand, when I see that page I can know, "Great, I can work with you." Transparency and honesty is important. You don't want to force an influencer to do something they are uncomfortable with and as an influencer you don't want to do something that is out of your wheelhouse because it's going to be uncomfortable for everyone. **–Jennifer Winberg, Marketing Consultant**

Call and ask for a free product or for free samples. Pretty much every brand is going to be willing to give you something to try out their brand so that's one of the best ways to reach out. Introduce who you are, say that you are really excited about their product and want to try it. **– Cynthia Rojas, Hype Digital Marketing**

It's really important for influencers and brands to align on core values for the best results. **–Peter Abraham, Content Marketing & Branding Expert**

Q: If an influencer doesn't have any kind of relationship with brands, where does an influencer go to start that dialogue and connect? What are the options available?

Get out there and go to events. Blogger was the catalyst for that. That was the beginning of it where they said, "Let's provide tools and resources for bloggers through these events" and as an agency, I wanted to go to these conferences to meet these people because I was trying to find these individuals and work with them so I cannot stress enough that despite this digital and social world, so much happens in a conversation over coffee or lunch. So, it's worth that money to go to those conferences where the brands are at. Look at their website, see who is going to be there, and target the brands that you want to work with. If a brand is doing a promotional booth, then more than likely the brand promotional manager is going to be there. **– Jennifer Winberg, Marketing Consultant**

On the brand side, I am always looking for influencers who are great content creators that I can co-create with or piggyback on to their tribe and their content. If you are out there creating compelling content whether it's a blog, whether you are speaking or its experiential or its video or social, if you have a strong point of view you are going to attract brands into your ecosystems. Every person and every brand is a media company now so it's really important to get out there and start creating. **–Peter Abraham, Content Marketing & Branding Expert**

I'm looking at content in the trucking industry for a client and the range of user-generated content is very wide in terms of the quality and I'm gravitating to the YouTubers that have six GoPros on their truck and they are doing some cool editing. **–Tony Winders, Winders Consulting Group**

As a blogger, it is really great to network in these private Facebook groups, but you have to be careful because what you think is private usually isn't. A lot of the people who are pitching to you are in the industry as well. We also belong to those groups as well. Make sure that you are professional online and not badmouthing these agencies that you are working with because it can affect your opportunity for a campaign. **–Tanya Salcido, UC Irvine Health**

Q: Will audiences always put up with influencer marketing?

The FTC just recently passed a rule now to address that. When someone is actually getting paid to represent something, that has to be communicated somewhere. I think people are very much aware and this is definitely a new space so we are starting to see more controls on what can and cannot be done so that people understand when someone is getting paid for influencer marketing. **–Cynthia Rojas, Hype Digital Marketing**

From the brand side, when I am building relationships with influencers, I always prefer people who are actually doing real things whether they are an athlete, chef, filmmaker, artist, whatever it is. People who are really doing something real other than saying, "Well, I've really got a tribe here. I kind of gamed the system and I'll sell it to you." That's really not interesting to me. **–Peter Abraham, Content Marketing & Branding Expert**

Q: What is the influencer/brand partnership like?

I don't really think in terms of influencers with brands, I think in terms of relationships. You have relationships at many different levels from an individual customer to a highly paid professional and everything in between. I think the strongest brands have really strong relationships with their tribe. They really build a tribe and when a brand has strong guard rails and they know what they stand for then it's really easy for a customer to go, "Yeah, not my brand," which is great. Every good brand needs guard rails. If you think of the brands that you like, they relate to you on a certain level, on certain channels, and you share values. If you are on the influencer side, you should be going to brands and going, "What can I do for you?" and if you are on the brand side, you should be going to influencers and going, "What can we do for you?" **–Peter Abraham, Content Marketing & Branding Expert**

If you are an influencer, you need to think about relationships in the long-term, it's not just campaign-specific. You never know because the person that you are interacting with could be at an agency six months later and they are going to remember what you did before. **–Tanya Salcido, UC Irvine Health**

The best influencers that we have partnered with do consider it long-term and are willing to partner with the brand to come up with content that is going to be over an extended period of time. Ultimately when somebody is going to make a purchase decision of any kind, typically they need more than one touchpoint. So simply doing one post isn't really going to get a brand too much influence. The influencers that we have partnered with who are really willing come up with a campaign strategy or tactical plan

are ultimately the ones who are the most successful. **–
Cynthia Rojas, Hype Digital Marketing**

**Q: Do you think influencers need to understand
marketing?**

Yes, 100%. I mean ultimately, they are a brand and are
marketing themselves. The ones that are super successful
understand that they are a brand, they understand who
their target audience is, they really truly understand the
marketing principles and are really quite savvy at it. **–
Cynthia Rojas, Hype Digital Marketing**

Brand-Influencer Fit

How to develop an influencer strategy that truly connects influencers with your values and your audience

Here are some key takeaways from the Brand-Influencer fit panel:

- **Trust is key**
  As a brand, it is important to trust the influencers that you work with. Understanding your influencer's personal brand and audience and ensuring that aligns with your target customer is the first step in building brand-influencer trust.
- **The brand message doesn't need to come from the brand**
  Recently brands have shifted their content creation process to allow influencers to share the brand's message in their own voice. When you allow influencers to have total control over the brand message you will find an increased connection between that message and your target audience.
- **Work with influencers who tangentially fit your brand**
  Working with influencers who may not be a direct fit with your brand can open up your brand to new demographics. This is very beneficial for brands looking to target a new market.

We are in an interesting time, where influencers are now having in some cases more reach than mainstream media outlets. One of the world's most venerated news outlets, the New York Times has about 30 million followers on Twitter, influencer Kim Kardashian has 47 million. It's an interesting time for influencers and influencer marketing. **–Josh Levine, The Rebel Group**

Q: Why are we here talking about fit? We don't have that conversation with other types of media. Why is fit so important with influencers and influencer marketing?

Fit is an interesting word because, over the last two years, influencers have been treated like any other channel. This is coming to a quick end as we get more analytics from platforms and we start to understand how to work with them better. I think it is most relevant because if we don't quickly shift to bringing influencers into the fold of the brand almost as guest creative directors, we start to run the risk of wasting time and effort on something that consumers sort of get, "Here try my product, take a picture and post it on your Instagram, here is a hashtag." We are sort of ending that era and entering this time where influencers come in and actually create content without direction from the brand or agency so fit becomes very important, both personality and who the audience is. **–Nick Kinports, Notice**

Margo and Me is a well-known fashion and travel blogger that we have worked with over the years with Peninsula–a really high-end luxury travel brand. She was looking to travel the world and we were looking to have an influencer talk about our brand so we got in a room, we chatted about ways that we could authentically fit into her travel plans. We are moving away from this one-and-done model where an influencer does one post and it's over. It's more about creating these ongoing collaborative relationships. **–Jennifer DeAngelis, Murphy O'Brien Public Relations**

One of the biggest changes in today's society is that a brand's message doesn't have to come from the brand anymore. When we think about these influencers, they are telling your brand's story in a way that might be a little different from your brand, but in a way, that might be more connected to how your customers are actually using your products if you find the right ones. In my opinion, the reason that fit is so important is because the influencer's expertise and their overall relationship with their fan base is such a big part of the "influence" and it isn't always taken into consideration when choosing influencers to work with. **–Kyle Wong, Pixlee**

Q: What impact does it have if you go to dinner with an influencer for the brands that you are working with? How does building genuine relationships with your influencers make a difference?

We focus on working with influencers who aren't just trying to make a dime, who understand what their brand is, and can have an open dialogue with us where they will say, "That's not a fit for me" or "That's going to help me a lot." We like working with people who are honest about who they are and what their brand is. **–Jennifer DeAngelis, Murphy O'Brien Public Relations**

When I look at the brands that have some of the best influencer-brand relationships, at the core of a lot of these relationships is trust. Trust often comes with great fit, it comes with nice personal relationships, but trust is so important because when you are collaborating especially in a creative environment when these influencers are tremendous creative storytellers, you need to have that trust because there is going to be differences of opinion and while you do need to provide some structure, you also need to let that influencer tell that story in an authentic way that resonates with his or her audience. Without that trust, I see a lot of fighting, a lot of disagreements, a lot of issues associated with this content being produced. **–Kyle Wong, Pixlee**

Sometimes it's as simple as looking back historically and finding out if an influencer has ever spoken or mentioned your product. If you want someone to represent a product, find out if they have ever mentioned your product in their social ecosystem historically because it ties back to the authenticity piece. **–Marissa Nance, OMD USA**

Q: How do data analytics and metrics work with influencer marketing?

I think the human aspect of building criteria before taking ideas to your client is super important, because the social media platforms themselves don't like tools. Some of them work with them, some of them don't. Every vendor that I have ever had come to us says, "Oh, we have great relationships, we have API visibility, we have everything that we need to dig into the data." It's just not true. Instagram doesn't give away its data and it doesn't let third-party companies view its data. You should know that because you really need to understand that there is no elegant way to do this and it has always paid us, many times over, to go in and do the time-intensive digging because it's well worth it. – **Nick Kinports, Notice**

We use social listening tools with our hotel brands so that we can see when influencers are coming to the hotel. We then ignited what was called a "Surprise and Delight" campaign where we would send them specialized amenities, discovered from stalking their Instagram page. A lot of times this opened the door for us to say, "We would love to invite you for a host experience" or something similar provided we saw an uptick in followers or traffic. – **Jennifer DeAngelis, Murphy O'Brien Public Relations**

Q: What are the tools and the processes that people should be using? What are some of the tactical tips to counter the complexity?

Some tools can help identify influencers that are maybe not so obvious to your brand. A good example of this happens in the outdoor industry a lot of the influencers are incredible ski enthusiasts and pro skiers, but most of their audience does not fall into this small niche pro skier demographic. Their demographic is the everyday person like me who make up a lot of their business and quite frankly, can't relate to the stories told by these really great impressive skiers. However, they can relate to the influencer who is talking about skiing as a great family trip, or a great way to connect with teammates.

Brands get so caught up in finding a fit that is directly related to one brand, but sometimes there are these influencers in these other tangential areas that are actually very beneficial to helping brands attract a different market, but more importantly making your brand more accessible to a different demographic. **–Kyle Wong, Pixlee**

Tactically, if you have your strategy and you know what you want to do then the next step is figuring out how you can bring it to life. Looking at this from an elevated perspective, you should now have engaged with a lot of people who are influencers. You need to create a dialogue and figure out how you extend their reach and be beneficial to them so let's not forget tactically we can look at the things that we do as well. **–Marissa Nance, Director, OMD USA**

Content Calendar Strategies

Learn how to plan your editorial calendar to create engaging content that grows your following. Learn simple tips you can use to plan your campaigns.

Here are some key takeaways from this panel:

- **Focus on creating quality content**
  Volume shouldn't be the focus of your content, instead, craft your content so that it provides value to your readers. Also, ensure that the content you are sharing is relevant to your brand.
- **Adjust the content for the platform**
  Whether you're creating a blog post, an email series, a YouTube video, a tweet, or an Instagram post, it's important to remember that each channel has a unique community that you need to cater your content to.
- **Establish a content creation strategy**
  Content creators, especially those who work on a team, should focus on streamlining the content creation process. Also, having all of your content assets in a central area for your team to access is very beneficial to your collaboration process.

Q: What are some of the best practices for brands and content calendar strategies? What is calendar fatigue?

I have had the pleasure of working with a lot of companies and their social media plans, and it's an exciting industry to be part of. People get excited when they hire a content team and they hire a social media marketer and they want them to be active at creating amazing content. Sometimes that ambition overlooks what is right for your brand. For us, it's always "go back to the brief." What are your brand's pillars? What do you believe in? What do you own and does that mean that you should be taking your logo and building it out of donuts and posting it to every channel just because it's National Donut Day? It's not about volume of how many tweets did you get this week or how many Instagram posts did you post this week, it's about the quality and the relevancy to your brand's pillars and is that message really important to your audience and to the themes that you believe in as a company. **–Kyle Snarr, Flipboard**

As a consumer, being bombarded with branded content on a daily basis, especially around big events like Halloween or Easter, I don't want to see another brand jumping on the holiday bandwagon. I think through everyone doing it, it lessens the impact. I think being strategic or tactical about when you are going out with these kinds of messages is important.

One really amazing example is American Express on Small Business Day. They basically created their own small business day because it didn't exist. I think the first year it did really well but it ended up going to Parliament and they created a petition to make it an official day and now Small Business Day is in the governmental calendar and that is how successful that campaign was. **–Lauren Sudworth, Hootsuite**

Q: Balancing popular and highly searched content with original content is important. How do you do that? How do you plan out your content?

It's all about having a mix of what people want to see and what you want to make. As a content creator, you have to stay authentic to yourself. The best ideas are the ones that are original, creative, and different from what everybody else is doing. When you can find those things, you can make an event out of it.

You need to balance sprint events vs. marathon series. Shark week is an example of a sprint week where people get really excited about it, it takes a lot of time to prepare for it, but once you do it–that whole week is moving and the momentum is going. You also have to have a marathon series where you do some sort of consistent content maybe once a week, once a month, but something that makes people want to come back and know when to come back as well. **–Aileen Xu, Lavendaire**

Every type of calendar strategy that you are going to create is going to be different for each platform that you are using. You can't blanket this across the board because each community is very, very different.

I find too frequently that brands will either repost stuff to their platforms or they don't really know how the community talks on that platform. There is an entire subreddit called "fellow kids" about brands who don't know how to talk to people they are trying to talk to and it's actually really worth looking up because it will show you what not to do along the way. **–Ty Stafford, Omelet**

Q: What tactical tools do you use that maybe other people are not using or are overlooked?

I've used a myriad from GatherContent to Contently.com to Google Docs, and I think it's more about the collaborative process between the content team and the blog team. The content team really needs to own the content that they are creating, brainstorm the topics and then work on the content that they are creating. That just means we get better quality content because what they are writing is what they are actually passionate about. We also use Google Spreadsheets, a blog, and Facebook at Work for posting results. The blog team posts the results back to the writers in long-form article content, which is perfect for our audience of writers because they are going to read through that and get everything that they need to know on last week's results in order to inform the next brainstorm. Wrike is a project management tool and all of our projects go through that as well. We use it with a combination of Google Docs. **–Lauren Sudworth, Hootsuite**

Anyone on any given team regardless of the size wants to see different things most of the time. For pretty much every content calendar that we create, we have folders for the project that includes those things such as the actual goals so if we have an assistant working on it and they were not at the meeting where we talked about the goal, then they can go look at that folder so they understand what is going on. I'm huge on making sure that we have photos or videos on every single thing that we post so we save those all in the same place and make sure that the edited versions on there so we know everything is setup properly. We do it all in Google Drive and then schedule through Epoxy, which is kind of the Hootsuite for video. **–Jane Davidson, BEGIN**

Tubular Labs for YouTube is a cool tool that I found for analytics. It goes deeper into your fans. It shows you your top fans, your most influential fans (which is really great for knowing who you might want to collaborate with because they already like your stuff and they are influential), and also it shows you who your fans are watching including their top videos and their top channels that they subscribe to so it is very useful for me as a creator. **–Aileen Xu, Lavendaire**

At my last agency, we had a subscription to Percolate and it was great because everything that went out needed to get approved and it has a great built-in approval system. You publish to Percolate and then everyone gets an email blast of what that piece of content is whether it is a blog post, image, or tweet and they can weigh in with feedback as well as approve or reject. They also have a very cool native mobile app that allows people to submit their own images, moments, quotes from work and places them in line for approval so it allows people to become part of the publishing process. It's legal-team friendly. **–Kyle Snarr, Flipboard**

HYPR is awesome. If you are going to have an influencer running your Snapchat or another platform, it allows you to get the analytics of that particular influencer, find out who they are and what general topics their audience is interested in. That data, as far as I know, is very difficult to get a hold of and this is the first group that has ever been able to offer me that. I've been using it like crazy both to identify audiences and to identify the influencers that I'm looking for. **–Ty Stafford, Omelet**

7 Examples of Effective Content from Hootsuite

Presented by:
Lauren Sudworth, Sr Content Strategy Mgr., Hootsuite

We need a definition of content before we can define effective content because in an organization or in a brand there are a lot of departments creating or commissioning content and not everyone follows the same process. Sometimes people see content as the words on the page and sometimes people see content as visual content or video content. We are often working towards different or conflicting goals and sometimes what we're asked for is not right for the brand or our customers.

Providing a clear definition of what content is helps you create the quality content that your customers (and your brand) deserve. Content can be anything: a song, a story, or the small part. What these all have in common is that they are all structured information. Content is structured information, but what we need to focus on is effective content.

Effective content provides a clear value to both the brand and the customer, has an intention and has value as a standalone asset, needs to be unique and credible to the brand it comes from (are you doing something else that isn't just a rip-off of another campaign or another brand's work? and are you proud of it?), and it needs to function as part of

---

the brand's ecosystem that encourages consumers to engage further by driving them elsewhere.

One example of this would-be Cards Against Humanity on the FAQ page. The brand answers questions in the same spirit of the game. They have a suggestion box where you can submit your "bad idea" and a "contact us." Their page is effective because it does have a value to the brand and their customer because they get fewer annoying emails and I got a belly laugh out of their answers. It works as a standalone asset because all of my questions are answered here and if not, I can contact them. It is definitely unique to the brand because no one else could get away with this level of "abuse" on their FAQ page and its definitely part of a connected ecosystem because there is a content button and a phone number.

Do less and do it better is the way to go and remember it all comes down to your audience. Whenever I put a new content strategy together, I think about where is the audience, who are they, and what do they want? I think running channel audits and understanding whether your audience is on Facebook or Snapchat is an obvious differentiator and it's not always what you think it is. There are new statistics coming out now that Snapchat is already beginning to age and so the highest growth for Snapchat is the 24-35 market whereas six months ago, that would have been under 18. So, I think running regular channel audits is super important and if you don't have huge budgets then honing in on a couple of places where your customers are most likely to be is key. Being specific is the most important thing you can do for your audience.

In conclusion, seven lessons summarized for you:

1. Get the basics right
2. Give old formats a fresh coat of paint
3. Innovation doesn't always mean what you think it does
4. Just because it's advertising doesn't mean it's not content too
5. Sponsored content can do wonders for your brand
6. Sometimes you need to put your product away and focus on other needs
7. Only your customers can tell you if your content is effective

Audience Question: How much is too much content to where you are losing your audience and losing your brand messaging? Where do you draw that line?

Answer: In the past couple of years where we have gone from brands trying to create good content to hitting that quality mark and there is a huge volume of content needed. I think a lot of times it's about bringing the volume down and focusing on targeted, specific, very high-quality content. One thing I look at is user rates. A lot of content in your ecosystem, sometimes, has no one looking at it. I think taking a neutral critical hard look at your content ecosystem and running a content audit to understand what is and isn't being used, then building an editorial calendar based on that information is the way that I would go about it.

5 Tips to Engaging Influencers Organically

Presented by:
Tim Sae Koo, Co-Founder and CEO at TINT

A common problem for brands occurs when there isn't a budget to pay influencers, but brands want to be able to use influencers regardless. Another problem is that canned paid influencer posts feel exactly like canned, paid influencer posts. The solution is well strategized, organic relationship building that occurs before there is a "need" for an influencer or a "need" for content.

There are a variety of influencers available starting with the A-list celebrity influencer who has millions of followers and is very expensive for brands to get. Typically, A-list influencers charge anywhere from $10,000 to $20,000 a post. Then there are power-middle influencers who have a following of anywhere from 10,000 to about 250,000 that are very niche in their industry and they have these intimate communities. The benefit of working with power-middle influencers is that they really resonate well with their audience and their audience really listens to them. There is a trend going into these power-middle influencers instead of the A-list and B-list celebrities because these power-middle influencers are so passionate about their niche topic that it can drive more engagement.

Here are 5 tips to help you build an organic long-term relationship with influencers, as opposed to a short-term transaction that is a "come and go."

Curate targeted content

Help influencers and make their job easier by curating content and sending it to them without anything in return. Give something without expecting anything in return. There are a couple of tools that I have used that can help you automate this process but still provide value including Pocket, Pinterest, and Twitter as well as Flipboard, IFTTT, and LinkedIn Pulse. These tools make it possible to find great content and then curate it into lists that you can send out to influencers that you want to connect with.

Band together for a cause

Partnering with charitable efforts will often naturally bring in other influencers that are interested in helping to shed light on a charitable cause. The intention of doing good by the brand can make it easier to connect with influencers and get them on board if they support the cause naturally.

Help influencers grow their presence

Invite your influencers to develop their brand. Focus on helping them grow their brand through their base audience and through their engagement. An example of this would be allowing an influencer to "take over" your brand Instagram so they can grow their audience while acting as the face of your brand.

Consider partnering with an influencer for an exclusive product launch

Partner with an influencer and launch products on behalf of their brand to their audience. It's a step-up from giving a discount code or a coupon code. When you find a way to launch a product or service that can be done with the influencer's brand, then that is great.

Meet in person

Schedule reach outs to meet in person and solve problems. I think emails are so easy but meeting in person, even for fifteen minutes, can be a powerful way to connect as well as build a real relationship that feels authentic.

Other ways to engage with new influencers:

- Acts of random kindness
- Create discount codes for audiences
- Invite only exclusive events
- Light, consistent social media engagement
- Reply to content with thoughtful commentary

People want to connect with people who show an interest in them so light consistent social media engagement and replying to content with thoughtful commentary shows that you are interested in that person and their brand. Influencers will remember this type of interest when a brand comes to them later on looking for an influencer.

5 Tips to build that organic long-term relationship vs. a short-term transaction that is a "come and go."

1. Targeted Content
2. Band Together for a Cause
3. Grow Their Presence
4. Exclusive Product Launches with the Influencer
5. Humanize in Person

Multi-Post Campaign Design

Whether you're posting a few YouTube videos or blog posts learn how to host an authentic branded campaign

Here are some key takeaways from this topic:

- **Keep campaign briefs to one page**
  Influencers, like most of us, are incredibly busy. Help streamline the process of your influencer campaign by ensuring that your campaign brief doesn't exceed one page.
- **Tailor the campaign content for each platform**
  Consider which platforms you will be publishing content on before starting your influencer campaign. Begin to craft your content based on the platform it will be published on, for example: repurpose long form blog content for Facebook, utilize Twitter for influencer Q&As, and create square images for Instagram.
- **Measure earned media**
  Track CPM on paid networks to showcase your campaign's ROI. Almost always, when you measure earned media from an influencer campaign vs traditional advertising, influencer campaigns have a higher ROI.

Q: What tools and resources do you use to run campaigns and find influencers?

I've been working with influencers for four years and back then we used good old Google Spreadsheets. Now we use platforms such as Group High to reach out to influencers and make connections. **–Tanya Salcido, UC Irvine Health**

We decided to give brand friendly influencers, the people who we want to attract, 25 ideas on what to blog about in August. We sent these out to our 4,000 influencers and said "Here are some ideas," and they forwarded it on to their friends and their friends clicked back to read it, and we had a pop-up that said, "Click here to join our influencer network." We actually get a lot of influencers by helping influencers. **–Josh Ochs, Media Leaders**

Define your objectives and don't bite off more than you can chew. Generally speaking, you never want to do more than five platforms for a campaign because it just gets crazy. As far as analytics, there are a ton of different things out there that you can use to measure whether it is Epoxy or Hootsuite. **–Alan Reed, TEN: The Enthusiast Network**

Q: What is a good length for a brief? Should we be sending out pages to influencers?

We got a brief from a big brand that a lot of us know and it was 3-4 pages long. I thought it was too long to be honest. If you are going to have a brief for influencers that work with you, we are all busy, so keep it to one page. **–Josh Ochs, Media Leaders**

Q: What are some best practices that can be done ahead of time to align expectations with the brand, to set up tools to track posts and to make sure that the influencers know what to expect to run a smooth campaign?

The biggest mistake is seeing the same type of content on different platforms. I don't think it works. I would like to see brands/companies/agencies harness the different social platforms and treat them differently. If you are going to post a blog, go to Facebook. If you are going to use Twitter, why not turn it into a Q&A platform where you have someone actively answering questions. **–Sarah Virk, BEGIN**

We did a project with Healthy Choice recently and we did the following thing: first of all, we had to internally go through processes. You need to know what your process is–what your 20 steps are because there are probably 20 steps to everything–whether you are an influencer network or a brand. I think a lot of people forget to think through the process. If you give your product out for free, what if they don't like it? What do you do if they don't get it? You have to plan, communicate, and be prepared. One tool that we love to use is what we call "the scrappy dashboard." We take a Google spreadsheet that we update and work on live, and we publish it to a web page, just that one tab, and we send the long link to the client so they can see that one tab. We were able to put all these blogs that we worked on with all these metrics in this colorful document: when they are due, when they are posting, we need approval, here is the following, here are the tweets, etc. The brand told us, "The scrappy dashboard is so helpful, we check it every morning. We love seeing where we are on the campaign." **–Josh Ochs, Media Leaders**

Flipboard is a place that bloggers or brands can go to tap an audience that they are likely not tapping right now. We have this high-quality, very influential, very active, and affluent audience. So when you have your campaign out and running, if you are looking for that extra traction or you are looking for that niche audience who loves that particular topic or brand or product, we have it. We work closely with bloggers to extend their outreach and they are paired next to high-quality content from the world's best publishers. – **Kyle Snarr, Flipboard**

Audience Q: What about marketing automation platforms and analytics for the whole customer journey? Are any of you using that as a research platform for your content?

The one single metric that we report to clients that gets them to spend more was earned media value. These clients have platforms where they are looking at how their campaigns perform side by side so for influencer campaigns and blog campaigns we do impressions times CPM on a paid network. So, if a YouTube view is $0.10 for a pre-roll ad and we got 100,000 YouTube view that is $10,000 in earned media value. Providing them this earned media value metric made them so comfortable that their campaign was getting an ROI because it is apples to apples comparison on how many impressions do these posts get me, how much would I normally pay to buy these impressions, and therefore we can show them that we got an ROI. **–Jesse Leimgruber, NeoReach**

Q: What are some ways that you position influencer and social campaigns to other channels and capture the value over time?

We often include a Millward Brown brand index study with all of our campaigns so you take a baseline at the beginning, because ROI is hard to show. With this in place, you can show the brand impact over time, which usually translates in the minds of the marketer or the CEO that there is an impact. Brand impact studies are kind of expensive, but it is a part of most campaigns that we run on Flipboard. **–Kyle Snarr, Flipboard**

Influencer Marketing Campaigns into eCommerce Results

Presented by:
Kyle Wong, Pixlee, CEO

There are a few things that have kind of changed in the market over the last few years that make things more applicable to marketers today. One is the fact that the amount of sharing has grown exponentially; there are 3.2 billion photos being shared each day. The scale has grown significantly. When we think about word of mouth marketing today, it is much more scalable because of social media. Today your customers are like media companies and they have a certain reach. It's no longer one person telling their neighbor what kind of sugar they like, it's one person telling the world what kind of sugar they like. The value of their advocacy is greater and the brand's story doesn't have to come from the brand. Another is that authentic customer content or visuals, as a whole, lead to sales and greater consumer engagement. Therefore, influencer marketing impacts multiple parts of the traditional customer journey.

Use unique coupon codes
One easy way to tie influencer marketing conversion to e-commerce success is to use coupon codes or set up an affiliate marketing program with the influencers.

Consider implementing a review program
Knowing your average order value can help determine how you can best use influencer marketing campaigns to your advantage. If you are a more expensive average order value brand, influencer marketing can be incredibly helpful when

it comes to getting someone to purchase. The more expensive a brand is, typically the more time it takes for the consumer to make the decision to purchase. An example of a company that uses influencer marketing really well is Rent the Runway. They have a review program where they use user-generated content to drive conversions by providing customer photos on real people and reviews. For a less expensive average order value brand, it's more about an impulse buy so you need to inspire people to purchase your product. Posts need to be more inspirational and aspirational.

Offer alternative perspectives of your brand

Perception is key. You will have some early adopters but there will come a point when you have to expand beyond that core audience in order to get new growth. That could be international, that could be customer segments, different brands, etc. You can use influencers to change the story of your brand by providing alternative perspectives of your brand and bring in new consumers who relate to this new story told by your influencers.

Turn your founders into micro influencers

Explain the why, beyond the what, and share your brand story with your consumers. This is especially important if you are an up-and-coming brand. They turn their founders and owners into micro influencers to drive conversions and share their story with their consumers. They share the founder's story to build legitimacy for the brand and for new products.

Find ways to help influencers

You also want to think about how you can help your influencers. Maybe you have a strong email list and you can push your influencer's content to your audience. Being able to push that influencer content to a different demographic is very valuable to a lot of influencers, simply for the exposure.

5 Ways to Monetize Your Content

Presented by:
Josh Hoffman, Digital Marketing Consultant,
JoshHoffman.com

Content marketing has been around for hundreds of years. If anyone remembers the Michelin Guide, it was created in the early 1900s. Recently, content marketing has become more of a buzzword expedited by social media. We are also now not competing with just other brands or competitors or other people in the industry, but we are literally competing with every other person.

You can go on Facebook right now and you will see something from your mom, something from Toyota, and something from your best friend...in that order. So, the rules of the game have completely changed. By 2020, they say the amount of content on the Internet is going to increase by 500%.

We need to change the way that we are approaching content creation.

These are the three key ingredients that I always use when creating content:

1. **Relatable:** The way that you relate to your brand is not the way that consumers relate to your brand. We love our products, we love our services, and we know the intricacies of them. When you know these details,

you appreciate the brand more, but the average person doesn't know that and they don't really care. They care about what your products or services represent. There is a great quote by Jay Baer, where he says, "If your stories and your content are all about your products, then that isn't a story, it's a brochure." Make the story bigger.

2. **Relevant:** Ask yourself if your content is really relevant to the people who you are trying to reach.

3. **Entertaining:** The reason I say that is if you look at digital media trends since 2008, in 2008 people were consuming digital media about 30 minutes to an hour a day. 2012 it's three hours a day. Today it's six. So, you went from 30 minutes to an hour to six hours. Your content has to be entertaining because that is what people want.

The definition of a media company is that their product is their content. The value of their content is directly correlated to the size of their audience. The bigger your audience is, the more your content is worth. That is why the New York Times can charge much more than Boise Chronicle. You need a big audience and big engagement for the highest monetization.

These are five ways that you can use to monetize your content:

1. **Native Advertising:** The actual ad fits the format of the channel or platform. It's not off to the side as a banner or a pop-up. If it's on NYTimes.com, it's an

article. If it's on YouTube, it's not the pre-roll ad, it's the video. When you grow big enough, brands will come to you to actually create content with you.

2. **Collaborative Content:** This means that you are going to work with non-competing businesses to share in the production and potentially the distribution of content. A podcast would be an example of this where you could launch a podcast and then take on the role as the host, but at the same time, you are going to work with non-competing businesses who want to reach the audience that you have and are willing to split the cost of producing and distributing that content.

3. **Traditional Advertising:** Native advertising is becoming more and more prevalent, but there are always going to brands that will say, "I don't have the budget for that, give me the banner ad." Traditional advertising is still very much alive.

4. **Affiliate Marketing:** Affiliate marketing is about creating relationships with people and brands. If you have a built-in audience that trusts you, you can say "Hey, go to Jenni Smith who has the premiere online cooking course that you should take" and then you earn a percentage of the sales that Jenni Smith receives from your affiliate link. This is contingent on the size of your audience.

5. **Revenue Sharing Opportunities:** Facebook and YouTube provide revenue sharing opportunities to content creators. Facebook is newer, but if you are

using instant articles it is a lot more favorable. You can sell your own ads in instant articles or you can use their audience network. YouTube gives creators $1-$2 approximately (based on your industry) per 1,000 views.

6. **Treat Your Content Like A Product**
   People buy New York Times and other premium memberships to access exclusive content online. Take a lesson from the Times and treat your content as a product in and of itself.

Relevant Content in a News Feed Economy

Presented by:
Nick Kinports, EVP Strategy, Notice

Strategy 1: Stop building campaigns, start building in clusters of ideas.

It's okay to have dramatically different ideas about advertising message as long as they all work up to one core principle. I think Geico is the best example that most people know. They run these TV ads that have no real connection between them so they were an early adopter of this cluster concept.

Strategy 2: Realize that the channel mix is also changing.

Events, photos and videos, and influencers are three core channel strategies. There is still definitely a place for broadcast television, out of home radio, etc. but the more bang for your buck is going to be in these three areas moving forward.

Strategy 3: Learn from Past Results

Continuous introduction of new content to the mix based on results and what has worked in the past can help you stay relevant in the news feed economy.

Strategy 4: Learn the platform roadmap

Facebook and Google are in a deathmatch for ownership of our newsfeed video, 360, and virtual reality. Everybody wants to own live video. Understand where platforms are going in the future because that can help you map out a strategy that will help our brands and our client's brands stay successful.

Strategy 5: Invest in events and experiences

Events create a nexus for influencers, customers, and rich content. In 2017, events and experiential marketing will be critical as social networks ratchet down organic search. Creating a purposeful and scalable events strategy will ensure every dollar is maximized when utilizing influencers and video content.

Q: It can be challenging getting people to attend the actual events so how do you overcome the challenge of getting the influencers to the event?

Well, if it's a budget challenge then that is tough because as you know, you do need some A-listers or some kind of headliner to anchor people and get them to participate. New product launches are always exciting. There is no easy solution, but I would say work with a core group of influencers to build cross-brand relationships so that they are more willing to work with you for less upfront because they know you are going to be bringing them the next thing next month and I think over time you can build some really wonderful relationships with them.

Develop the right publication skillsets. Publishers are dying and being replaced by influencers, platform-only publications, and niche groups. The interesting thing for brands is that they can develop and own a publication space with relative ease, impacting SEO, offsetting ad spend, and helping their customers keep their finger on the pulse.

Creating cool content and maintaining a news feed presence is biased towards the publication model, and brands know their industry best.

Do your own measurement work? Platforms are now walled gardens that don't play well with others and don't really want to play with others. Nobody has true real-time data from platforms so you need to become experts in each platform and then measure the tools that are available in there and then you need to create reports from that that are meaningful to your clients. Accepting 1:1 results between platforms are not measurable is the first step to being accurate, next is mastering niche skillets for measurement in each platform.

Q: Is there a sweet spot in your opinion of video length?

Probably ten seconds is what we shoot for as a core success element. If you think about telling the whole story in ten seconds or at least telling the core of that story in the ten seconds. Everything else is nice to have, but we won't probably be getting much out of it. For Facebook, Live though, you need something that is at least 15 minutes long. You need to be able to have a plan that allows you to capture at least 15 minutes because what is going to happen is that as you start that Live video, Facebook is going to send out notifications to everyone who likes your brand's page. Those notifications do not all happen at once and it sort of knows as more people watch to send out more notifications so the longer you can do, the better. We have done some that have been an hour length because 10 people come on, 30 people come on, 100 people and then it goes down to 90 and so people cycle in and out.

Brands Share Proven Influencer Marketing Strategies

Examples from successful campaigns and why they work from a brand perspective

Here are some key takeaways from this topic:

- **Connect with influencers that have the same philosophy as your brand.** Connecting with an influencer just because they have a large following may not be the best fit for your brand's campaign. Instead focus on finding influencers, with an engaged audience in your niche, who share the same values as your brand.
- **Consider partnering with influencers as a way to create engaging content.** Traditional content creation is typically slow and expensive, leverage influencers as a way to generate high-quality content for all of your brand's various channels.
- **Track influencer campaigns with unique offers codes.** Use unique offer codes to gauge the conversion rates of the different influencers in your campaign. Utilize these metrics to better understand which influencers had the widest reach, the most engaged audience and the highest conversion rates. This data allows you, as a brand, to determine which influencers to work with on future campaigns.

Q: How do influencer campaigns get conceived? Where does it happen in the organization of a marketing department when it comes to marketing plans and budgets?

I always start with the target audience mindset. Ultimately, a purchase or a consumer decision is always based on emotions. This being said, it is critical to understand not only the demographic of your target audience, but who they are from a psychographic and emotional perspective as well.

One of the brands that has done this really well is Jeep. Jeep was really able to tap into the insight that when people— think of Jeep they think of running wild and free, through the dunes, and going where no car can go. They speak to the audience's need for adventure and freedom. There is huge Jeep brand loyalty, and it is shown in the number of sites, blogs, Instagram's, and clubs dedicated to Jeep. The brand loyalty is because Jeep taps into their target audience emotional need. That is where I like to start with every brand. Once you understand the customer need, the brad story can unfold from there. **–Cynthia Rojas, Hype Digital Marketing**

I think it's interesting because organizationally, influencer marketing falls into a lot of different places. This is because influencer marketing is a tactic, a way to reach your customers and deliver a message. I think the common misperception in influencer marketing is that it is a magnet, just a way to get eyeballs. However, it is also effective at reaching new audiences and leveraging existing brands and influencers to build your own. At the same time, there are a lot of applications of influencer marketing that build loyalty, educate consumers, and get people through that consideration phase, into the conversion phase to actually buying your product. **–Andrew Higgins, Pixlee**

For me, high-volume influencers are not really the people I consider first. Going for influencers with huge followings is definitely one tactic for a brand-new product, however, I think of high volume influencers as only "semi-authentic."

This isn't disrespecting this type of influencer at all, but you also have to ask yourself, what are they actually experts in? Someone who isn't that passionate about your particular product or niche, but has a large reach is not as attractive to me as someone with 1,000 followers who knows everything about the subject. For these reasons, I wouldn't use influencer marketing personally to start a conversation, I would use it to close one. **–Seb Webber, Coldplay Inc**

Our brand is built on authenticity. When I talk about our influencers, I'm talking about guys like Mark Healy. Mark Healy is a high-profile sponsored athlete. He came to us. He said, "Look, I only wear your brand. I only wear OluKai. Let's work together." For us, that is the first signal when someone comes to us and says, "You fit my philosophy, you fit in my lifestyle." If it's anything other than that, we won't really talk to them because it's just not worth it. **–Kerry Konrady, OluKai**

We help brands make their marketing more authentic at Pixlee through real customers. A message no longer needs to come from the brand itself, and quite frankly, it's often a much stronger message when it doesn't. It's word of mouth.

You go back thirty or forty years, word of mouth was maybe someone talking to 20 to 30 people a day but today every consumer has the chance to be a media company. They have a giant megaphone in their pocket so the concept of micro-influencers, it's really just relationships. You can develop your brand through these relationships and when you are talking about influencers, it can't be a transactional relationship. It's not, "I pay you for your audience." It really is about going deeper and that comes down to picking the right influencers. If you have to alter the influencer to fit your brand, it won't work. **–Andrew Higgins, Pixlee**

We found that an up-and-coming neighborhood, was populated with more working class, and a creative class demographic and we hypothesized this customer segment would be price sensitive but still not want to cut their own lawns. So, we segmented those zip codes and only ran a specific ad for them, with a headline 'The Cheapest Lawn Mowing in Nashville. Lawn mowing from $20.'

We then created a matching landing page. After running the ad for one month we saw a 200% lift in the click through rate and a 30% lift in on-page conversion. Studying the data your own business generates can tell you which of your online marketing campaigns works best. Do the ads appeal to your target market or another market altogether? The data may also point to completely new areas of customer interest. **–Bryan Clayton, GreenPal**

Q: What are brands spending on YouTube stars and Instagram influencers? How is performance measured with influencer marketing?

There is a wide range in terms of the economics of it. There are quite a few influencers that I've worked with who are willing to take some sort of percentage backend deal, and those are typically influencers that have a smaller following. Oftentimes, these influencers have a really good understanding of their followers, and their followers are passionate and motivated. These influencers know when they recommend something that their followers are going to get on board with whatever they are saying.

The bottom line is that you can build an influencer program regardless of how small or large your budget is. Influencers who are younger are going to be more willing to partner and be flexible in their partnership, which is great for young brands. **–Cynthia Rojas, Hype Digital Marketing**

Those influencers, then, are promoting the brand in whatever way they want in many cases, which makes for a more authentic campaign. **–Tony Winders, Winders Consulting Group**

If it is purely about reach, then I look at partnering with influencers in the same way I would look at a traditional print ad or an online buy–a CPM, essentially. In your world, you know what those costs are and you negotiate against that.

The other way that I look at it is that an influencer is coming in and becoming almost a part of our organization similar to a full-time employee. This gets a little soft, but it is also similar to artists who I commission to work on our behalf, so they can continue to do your trade.

Right now, we are funding murals all over the country by artists. It's really less of a pay-to-play, as much as it is our brand helping these artists with their passions and then these artists helps to provide us with a passionate group of followers who care about what we are doing. **–Kerry Konrady, OluKai**

I'll be honest, it's still really hard to track this stuff. It's like that age-old saying, "50% of my marketing is working, I just don't know what 50%." There are metrics that you can view. I can tell if you have opened an email, clicked on it, been on a page for 17 seconds, etc. I can't tell if you actually go home and think about my stuff. I'll know if you buy it, but I won't also know if it's because of anything that I have done that you are buying it. **–Seb Webber, Coldplay Inc**

A big piece of this is that every marketer needs more content. There are just too many channels. Traditional content generation is really slow and it's expensive. I think what you are doing in partnering with these influencers is generating some really high-level and engaging content.

Another way to look at the value and track the performance is to look at the content metrics and channels that you are using to share that influencer content outside of social. **– Andrew Higgins, Pixlee**

One of the things that we have done is provide influencers with unique offer codes, and have developed separate landing pages for them so we can track their customer journey. This helps the brand quickly understand which influencers are driving the most traffic to the site and who is converting the most. **–Cynthia Rojas, Hype Digital Marketing**

One point that I would make to influencers is that I'm seeing more and more people start to market themselves and promote multiple brands, even competitor brands. It's becoming an issue for us because it waters down our message. It makes them less appealing to us when they are associated with a number of brands in our market. **–Kerry Konrady, OluKai**

Audience Q: How can the influencer educate a brand relative to quality vs. scale and relationship building vs. analytics and measurement?

Some of the influencers that I have talked to have developed marketing packages for themselves that showcase parts of their website, testimonials from people who are in their community, and this demonstration of efficacy has really helped them. These real examples help demonstrate the value and the quality that the influencer can provide. **–Cynthia Rojas, Hype Digital Marketing**

Want to know what customers see when they search for your brand online?

Our team works with brands of all sizes to ensure their brand message is Light, Bright and Polite.

Get a digital brand audit from our team to see how your customers are finding you (and what they think about your online footprint).

Visit MediaLeaders.com/Audit

Our online audit includes:
10 page customized report with your brand's online footprint
- We show you positive mentions that can be utilized for content marketing
- We highlight negative results and give you multiple suggestions on how to remove them
- We provide a custom video library designed to help your brand to improve its online footprint
- Also learn:
  - How content marketing can build a pipeline of prospects
  - Influencer marketing tips
  - Social media tips for reputation management
  - 5 key tips your brand can use to improve your online presence

Visit MediaLeaders.com/Audit to learn more

Part 3: Analyze

Once you've hit your stride creating exciting and engaging marketing/PR campaigns, it's the next step that makes all the difference–measuring their effectiveness. These panel discussions feature experts with valuable experience collecting and learning from the data.

A/B Testing Best Practices for Digital Marketers

A/B testing is the practice of comparing two variables to see which variable more effective at maximizing the desired outcome. For example, a web designer can A/B test two landing pages to see which page has a higher click-through-rate on an advertisement. Or, an email marketer can compare two email subject lines to determine which one has a higher open rate. Once you have a solid A/B testing strategy in place you can really start to create content that is optimized for engaging your audience and increasing conversions.

We asked 11 digital marketers, what are some must-know digital marketing best practices for A/B testing?

1. Segment your traffic for A/B tests

A lot of marketers run A/B tests without segmenting desktop and mobile, when in fact, that's probably one of the most important things to do for your results to be reliable. Sample size is important, but the thing is, you need to have a big enough sample size for both desktop and mobile. Some things work for desktop and don't for mobile and vice versa. So, if you don't segment desktop and mobile you might really miss out. **–Sergey Alakov, Humberview Group**

2. Set weekly goals

Each week set a new goal tactic that cannot overlap with other goals previously tackled. For example, week 1 = FB ads, week 2 = Leadpages and week 3 = affiliate program. The marketing techniques that are going to work for you all depend on your niche, your target audience, your geographical location, etc. To really know which will work for your business and which will not you have to trial and error. One week is a preferred time length for testing as it is long enough to implement the strategy and get results plus short enough to try multiple marketing techniques over a couple months' span. At the end of each month, look back at the marketing tactics you tried and look at your analytics (i.e. did your sales rise or decline? How many man-hours did it cost you to implement and manage that strategy? What was your engagement?). After answering those questions, you will have a pretty good idea of what techniques will work for your brand without having to use an expensive complicated software. **–Melissa Gosse, CanIRank**

3. Alter your images

If your brand is launching a new product or service, you have to know what your audience responds to better. A/B testing, whether it's through mediums like Facebook, Bing or Google AdWords', provides an excellent way to see what your customers really want. One tip is to alter your images. For example, have the text in the center of the image on test A and the text off to the side on test B. Something as small as text can yield surprising results. **–Tory Kalousek, Blue Compass**

4. Focus on the elements that have the biggest impact on conversion

Don't sweat the small stuff. Follow the Pareto Principle (also known as the 80/20 rule) and identify the 20% of your web-pages or communication pieces that generate 80% of your results. Then, when you design your testing strategy for those assets, focus on the elements that have the biggest impact on conversions, such as headline, sub-headline, images, and calls to action. **–Sarit Neundorf, Integrate & Automate**

5. Include a chat widget on your site
One A/B test to experiment with is including a chat widget on your website. Do users spend more time on your site when there is a chat box? Is it better to have the chat option pop up or hidden until users press a button?

A chat box allows for the first online interaction between a business and its customers. By testing different strategies, you can discover the ideal way to greet potential clients who are peering into your company's virtual window. **– Henry Butler, CanIRank**

6. Prioritize your tests
The key to testing is setting yourself up to get an actual ROI on your efforts. Avoid jumping in and running tests randomly. Always rank your potential tests by the level of effort to implement, potential impact, and confidence of impact, and regularly re-prioritize tests based on new ideas and results.

Bonus tip: Check out Behave for actionable ideas! **–Dylan Whitman, BVAccel**

7. Create a pre-test checklist

When you're first setting up a test, start by giving yourself a pre-test checklist. If you can't answer the following 4 questions, refine your campaign until you can.

1. What information are you hoping to learn from the test?
2. Which variable are you changing?
3. Can you generalize the test results? i.e. can you apply the learnings from this email to future emails, or better yet, can you apply it to other marketing efforts such as the design/UX of your website?
4. Is your test sample statistically significant?

–Amelia Willson, HostGator

8. Test one variable at a time

Don't make A/B Testing more complicated than it is. When it comes to testing, be sure only to test one variable at a time. If you're looking to get a better open rate, then begin with testing the subject line of your email. That's the first thing your audience is going to see and will make or break your campaign. If you're looking to increase the click through rate on purchases, then take a look at the content of your email. It can be many different things that affect your results. Take a look at the copy, images, font, buttons and other potential factors keeping you from getting the results you need. However, you don't want to test more than factor at a time. If you do so, you won't be able to find out where the source of the problem is and how to fix it. **–Kristian Rivera, Fit Small Business**

9. Get ideas from your competitors

A step-by-step approach to quick, performance-led A/B tests:

- Run search queries using keywords you and your competitor's target.
- Take the most highly ranked content and study it meticulously.
- Create your first test creative to match your competitor's as closely as possible, in structure, content optimization, and user experience.
- Then draft your second test creative using your own ideas.
- This is performance-led (your competitor is giving you the first creative). Monitor the first 1,000 visitors and discard losers quickly!

–Ali Khan, SatchCorp Ltd

10. Create dramatic variations between your tests

Don't run headline tests for too long if you're running them for 100% of your audience. Create dramatic variations between your tests. The more dramatic you make the changes the more likely you'll find a meaningful winner. If you find a winner in ~1 hour, implement the winner. If the experiment hasn't found a meaningful winner in an hour, pause the experiment and move on, trying more dramatic variations next time. Lastly, set meaningful goals for your organization. **–Allison VanNest, Parse.ly**

11. Study the data your business generates

Sometimes big data sources can be right at your fingertips. Leverage your data, combined with publicly available census data, for marketing insights to come up with A/B tests for landing pages and pay channels.

For example, in a recent campaign we ran in Nashville, TN, we ran pay-per-click (PPC) Adwords campaign with one ad targeting the entire metro Nashville area. The headline read 'Local Lawn Pros in Nashville are a click away.' and the performance of the ad was good with a click through rate of over 1% and conversion rate of over 10% on the Nashville landing page but we wanted to improve on it.

We set out to make our brand more contextual and relevant to the viewer. So, we researched census data, looking at the average income and home values throughout the Nashville area.

We found that an up-and-coming neighborhood, was populated with more working class, and a creative class demographic and we hypothesized this customer segment would be price sensitive other market altogether? The data may also point to completely new areas of customer interest. **–Bryan Clayton, GreenPal**

ROI on Social

Your brand wants to tap into the tremendous potential of social media but it's easier said than done. Our experts share their best insights on maximizing on social media, the tools they use and the importance of focusing on the metrics that increase conversions.

Here are some key takeaways from this topic:

- **Social ROI is not one size fits all**
  For many industries, social ROI can mean different things. How one brand measures social can be completely different than another brand. Understand your brand's goal on social to determine if your analytics measure up.
- **Keep an eye on your competitors**
  Social media makes it easy to see what your competitors are doing online. Find your competitors' case studies, try to learn from their successes, then differentiate yourself from them. Get creative on social and find unique ways to increase your ROI.
- **Avoid being product-centric on social**
  It's important for brands to avoid becoming product-centric with their messaging on social. People don't see themselves as consumers and if you create a buyer persona that is consumer driven and doesn't speak to your readers on a personal level then you will have low social ROI.

Q: What are the differences between vanity metrics and actual ROI? How do you use a mix of them?

I think the biggest trend that is happening is from an analytics perspective. Different analytics are tracking different behaviors in different spaces, but the biggest thing is figuring out how your analytics are lining up with your campaigns. Just saying "I'm going to track engagement over here and then I'm going to track conversion over here and they are not related," is not the right way to do it. You need to think about how your analytics are all connected. – **Jennifer Winberg, Marketing Consultant**

I would say the two biggest analytics that matter outside of actual money coming into your pocket is how big your audience is as well as how relevant your audience is. On top of that, is engagement. Understand how much time people are willing to give you on a day-to-day or a week-to-week basis. Time and attention are the two biggest currencies in the digital space because without people's time and attention, you are not going to touch their wallet. **–Josh Hoffman, JoshHoffman.com**

ROI is many different things to many different industries. It's not one size fits all. The way that a movie studio measures social in regards to ROI is a lot different than how an auto manufacturer uses social media to drive sales in a local dealership. The KPIs are always different. **–Sirous Wadia, GumGum**

Q: What is the role of competition in ROI, in measurement? How do you set the baselines and benchmarks against competitors?

A lot of it is just seeing what the brand's competitor is doing online. Thankfully with social media, you can definitely go out there and see what people are doing. The biggest thing is that you have to find a way to differentiate yourself. Keep an eye on your competitors and learn from their successes and failures as well. There are so many case studies out there for you to look at and people will publish the results so you can figure out whether you want to do something comparable. **–Jennifer Winberg, Marketing Consultant**

One of my favorite tricks is using bit.ly links to track competitors because if you put a "+" sign at the end of any bit.ly link, it will show you the metrics of that campaign. **– Serena Ehrlich, Business Wire**

Q: Do you create a persona for your company to guide your social strategy?

Think about who your persona is. What drives them. What their challenges are. What is hard in their life and what is easy in their life? How do they operate? How do they run? Think about the customer journey. **–Jennifer Winberg, Marketing Consultant**

Brands that have people in HR and research & development areas think that they don't need to know anything about social media, but every single person in your business or organization should have a basic fundamental understanding of not just social media but of all of the marketing. Marketing is your messaging, branding, content, how you talk to customers, how you receive feedback and circle that within your organization. When using a buyer persona, ensure that you are treating your customers as people and not just consumers. People don't look at themselves as consumers, they look at themselves as people who just happen to buy things for different reasons. When you make your social media so product-centric and service-centric, you end up talking to people as consumers and you turn people off. **–Josh Hoffman, JoshHoffman.com**

Q: Which social platform is providing the most ROI? Provided that you understand your audience and understand your content?

Brands with an online store can set up a Facebook conversion tracking ad and then Facebook will literally tell you "we drove this many people to the page, they bought the product and here is how much you made, how much you spent." The analytics are very clear. For the people that do not have an online store, use the revenue-sharing programs that both Facebook and YouTube provide to content creators. Everyone is a content creator whether you want to call yourself that or not. And the key to understanding how to take advantage of that, in addition to selling products and services, is to treat your content as one of your products and services. Marketing can then become a revenue source within the company. **–Josh Hoffman, JoshHoffman.com**

Q: What do you do when the C-Suite want the numbers, but you have to put in the time and content to get those numbers?

You must explain the process to the executives in your company and explain what it takes to turn around those numbers. When movie studios release a movie, they drop the first trailer a year in advance and the first poster, and they test it all. They test the reactions of the people to these initiatives and then they course-correct along the way. The CEO of that studio cares about the opening weekend, the second weekend, those opening numbers and box office results but that journey along the way over the course of that year to those initiatives is vital. You can't have one without the other. So, the CEO gets what they want, but there is a long building process to hit those numbers. **–**
Sirous Wadia, GumGum

Keeping Analytics Simple

What metrics to look for in your analytics to find out what content engages your readers. How to use this info to grow your influence

Here are some key takeaways from this topic:

- **Engagement is everything**
  The number one analytics number to pay attention to, is engagement. Brands with engaging content have better word-of-mouth and customer loyalty.
- **Facebook Ads have the best analytics**
  With Facebook having the largest audience and so much consumer data it is no wonder that businesses, small and large, are finding a lot of success with their Facebook ads. Consider using Facebook or Instagram for your next targeted ad campaign.
- **Score your content**
  Create a process and set of questions that you can use to score your content. When you create a content scoring process you will be able to see which content isn't performing well and why. Use that data to optimize your content for engagement.

Q: What metrics are out there to measure things that are not directly trackable with conversions?

I think that the number one analytic that everyone should pay attention to, whether it was four years ago, today, or four years from now is engagement. Engagement literally shows you who is paying attention to you, and therefore who cares about what you have to say. Everything else comes after that. If you are not going to grab people's time and attention in 2016 and moving forward, then you are not going to touch their wallet. They are not going to go to an ecommerce shopping cart. They are not going to walk into a store. They are not going to refer you to anyone and produce word-of-mouth. **–Josh Hoffman, JoshHoffman.com**

If quantitative analytics and engagement is the what, the qualitative is the why. So, after we have looked at the hard numbers, the bounce rates, the engagement rates, then the next thing we want to look at is why things are not performing well.

I think looking at a set of content principles or content questions that you can ask helps you score content. Out of the ten different dimensions that your content has–the context, the tone of voice, the visuals, how it responds on any device, etc., you can start to see where things are going wrong. I think a lot of people focus on how well written content is or how pretty it looks and there are a lot of hidden layers in UX and UI that go into creating a piece of content. **–Lauren Sudworth, Hootsuite**

When speaking with brands and influencers, I always ask, "What are your objectives?" There are thousands if not millions of things that you could measure, and you get bogged down in it, it doesn't work. **–Alan Reed, TEN: The Enthusiast Network**

Q: What channels are working the best and getting the best analytics? If someone is looking to run an ad, where are people going today?

I think the newest channel always works the best. You see a depreciation in click through rates as time goes on. When display ads first came into existence, everyone was clicking on them because they were new and exciting, and you could get a 3% click through rate, which would be insane these days. One of the latest things is content discovery like Taboola and Outbrain. **–Lauren Sudworth, Hootsuite**

Facebook has so much consumer data. I work with some small businesses on the consulting side and I think there is a lack of education in understanding how powerful the Facebook advertising platform is, which obviously is now accessed by Instagram. You can create such targeted campaigns and Facebook still has the biggest audience with the greatest reach among all of the ages, income rate, and multicultural groups. **–Josh Hoffman, JoshHoffman.com**

Facebook Power Editor gives you so much control and is a tool worth using. **–Jesse Leimgruber, NeoReach**

Q: What tools do you recommend for analytics, for social listening, for running campaigns, for creating better content?

I use Mention.com and it searches loads of keywords on Reddit, Quora, Everything, and Google Alerts is free. **–Jesse Leimgruber, NeoReach**

We use Hootsuite. My team enjoys that it is easy and fast for brand management. We also use direct Facebook insights and other listening tools such as Socialbakers and CrowdSocial. Getting direct insights from a platform is really valuable as well. **–Josh Levine, Rebel Group**

On Hootsuite, the inquiries can get you a long way. They are a really great way of doing the analysis at the beginning of the process with competitor analysis, then understanding what your customers are talking about either directly to you or about you, and then again at the end to see what went well. **–Lauren Sudworth, Hootsuite**

There are tools like Domo, Epoxy, Hootsuite, and many more. It really depends on what your goals are. **–Alan Reed, TEN: The Enthusiast Network**

You can get on the phone with a representative of any of these tools, and let them sell you the product. There are also usually free or short-term trials. If it doesn't work, most of these things are a monthly subscription system. Take the tutorials. It's not like a magic wand that you wave and it does it all for you. It's meant to assist. Also, when you are looking at tools and resources, think not just about the singular thing that it does but maybe the multiple levels of things that it does. **–Jennifer Winberg, Marketing Consultant**

Tactics for Simplifying Site Analytics

It's the fantasy of every copywriter and graphic designer to focus exclusively on producing beautiful, creative content and visuals without having to worry about site analytics. But for a business to succeed, you need reliable analytics to gauge your website's effectiveness and find out what's working (or not) in order to grow your influence, brand awareness, and ultimately your business. We asked experts for their best tips and tools for quantifying web presence and using the analytics to test and improve your strategy.

1. Quantify your web presence with organic search and linking domains

These days, most companies focus their search presence through paid channels. However, organic search is an exceptionally easy way to quantify your web presence. There is a tool we love called SEMrush that will crawl your website and provide your position for every single term that you rank for on Google. In addition, SEMrush shows you how your rankings have changed over time, month-to-month, and more.

This tool also provides estimated traffic and an estimated paid search savings that you can use to justify any time spent working on your website's SEO. It is perfect for small businesses that do not have the budget to pay for expensive marketing firms.

Your web presence can easily be quantified by the amount of linking domains that connect with your website. These links can easily be tracked in Google's Search Console or third party tools such as Ahrefs or Moz. **–Sacha Ferrandi, Source Capital Funding, Inc.**

2. Utilize the Navigation Summary in Google Analytics

One the best resources Google Analytics offers is the Navigation Summary, showing where visitors were before and after visiting pages on your site. View the CTR (click-through-rate) to desired pages within your conversion funnel using the Navigation Summary. To find it, click the Navigation Summary tab above the explorer graph on page-specific analytics reports.

The Navigation Summary shows you where users naturally want to click next and helps you form sound hypotheses about moving visitors throughout your website from various landing pages and conversion pages. These site analytics give you action items and tests to run that help quantify the optimization of your campaigns. **–Stephanie Grangaard, Blue Compass Interactive**

3. Use metrics like "time on site", "social shares" and "conversions" to measure user engagement

For many marketers, outlining and measuring key performance indicators (KPIs) is the key to success. One KPI at the top of the list should be user engagement. For those new to the game, if you want to learn how to create high-quality content that your readers will care about, it's very important to know how users have engaged with your content in the past in order to gauge how they may interact with your content in the future.

There are many different ways you're able to measure user engagement, but a few site analytics stand out to be true indicators.

- **Time on Site.** How much time are your readers spending on your website? If you have a 1000-word blog post and the average time on site for that particular page is 15 seconds, chances are your readers aren't getting too far past the first headline and opening sentence. Be sure you're writing content that applies to them and leaves them wanting more.
- **Social Shares.** This is a great way to know readers are engaging with your content. If your audience reads and loves your killer content, they'll share it. Just like that, you've spread your message beyond your audience to include all their friends (and their friends' friends, too).
- **Conversions.** There are many different conversion points on websites and social content, but an easy one is getting visitors to subscribe to your blog emails. This is a great way to measure your site analytics and how well your readers are engaging with what you're putting in front of them. If you find you have a really great week and are attracting tons of new subscribers–followed by a very slow week, or even lost subscribers–take a look at the site analytics and the type of content you were putting out between those two-time periods and analyze what worked with your audience and what didn't. It's a

good way to indicate how your readers are reacting to your hard work.

- **Use the tools that work for you.** There are many great resources available for measuring the success of your digital marketing efforts, but below are two of my favorites.

Google Analytics tracks and reports virtually every website metric you could think of. It's a great, free way to see how much traffic is coming to your site, where it's coming from and how your visitors are interacting with your pages. Just apply your universal tracking code snippet to your web page and start seeing data that matters.

Sprout Social is an excellent platform for measuring all of your social media efforts. Not only can you track and report on all of your tweets, Facebook posts or Instagram photos, you can also schedule content pushes to automate your social initiatives. While you can use the social insights that each platform offers for free, Sprout Social also offers more ways to effectively measure your efforts with ease for a little bit of a cost. **–Sean McCaffrey, PrimePay**

4. Optimize your content by looking at bounce rate, number of website visits and generated leads

Content plays a crucial part in customer engagement. The metrics used to analyze its effectiveness play an even more vital role. Some of the important metrics that can be quite useful in measuring the content's effectiveness include 1) bounce rate 2) number of website visits and 3) generated leads. A few of the preferred web analytics tools that offer effective metrics are Google Analytics, Raven, and Moz.

Constantly optimizing your content based on the insights from these metrics is an ideal way to grow your influence. – **Swapnil Bhagwat, Orchestrate**

5. Consider looking at a heat map of your site

Few small business owners use Crazy Egg. This tool shows a heat map of where your visitors viewed on a page if they scrolled to the bottom, and where they exited. Combine that data with how long they stayed on the page using Google Analytics, and you now have a good idea if your content engages and what visitors care about.

Other great resources include Google Webmaster tools to find out if you have any error pages, which will hurt you on Google. Finally, I use Sysomos which tells me what my brand sentiment is online and in social media. **–Clint Evans, StandOut Authority**

CRM Best Practices

Customer-relationship management begins with a simple concept: knowing your customer and putting that knowledge to work. Our experts share their best tips.

Here are some key takeaways from this topic:

- **Remember the end goal**
  Decide what Key Performance Indicators (KPI) you need to measure and why. Reserve your time and energy for data collection that is actionable.
- **Create accurate buyer personas, and use them to shape CRM practices**
  Ask them what they need, how they like to receive communications and do your best to accommodate.
- **Evaluate your practices and ask if there's a better way**
  Before you make a change, do a classic ROI calculation. What does your current system cost in dollars and manpower, and could a different solution improve upon that?
- **Have one central view of the customer**
  CRM is all about building relationships and nurturing those relationships as well as acquiring new relationships. Focus on putting all of your systems in one place so all of your team members are able to collaborate in one place.

Q: We can all agree that CRM is a sophisticated part of the stack; it is not easy by any means. Yet often I see clients underestimating how much work it takes. Where do you begin with CRM from the business, operational and technical perspective?

With relationship marketing, it focuses on the same concepts of literally any relationship whether it is personal or client. But with the advent of better technology and better data, it has become a requirement now for companies not just to project to 20 or 40 clients–now we are projecting to millions. I have worked with a lot of companies from Nestle to Disney and PlayStation, and it always comes down to three elements for me. First is your data that you are collecting about consumers or customers. Second is deciding what you do with it. And the third element is communication. If you piece those together, that is your $64 million-dollar solution. **–Nick Metcalfe, Saatachi & Saatachi**

I really recommend utilizing the data in a way that is actionable, and one of the best ways to do that is through persona marketing. It's taking that data and telling a story with it. Who are the people that you are talking to? What are their communication preferences? What are their challenges? Take all of that and wrap it up into a persona to help your sales and marketing teams speak to them in a way that is helpful to them. **–Ronnie Kassiff, Inbound Marketing Consultant**

From an enterprise perspective, it is important to set up project governance and requirements early on. Not just the

KPIs, but what are your use cases and what are the journeys that your customers can take? **–Marc Kravitz, Microsoft**

I would say build a people-based vision within your organization. Over the last few years, organizations have been very siloed, with whole departments focusing on search or affiliation. You want to have one single view at the end of the day to stay customer-centric such as building a department for the first visit or the first purchase. Building the vision–and then discovering how to get the right KPIs to measure the true performance–are critical. The key takeaway here is incrementality: how to build and measure true incrementality at the people-based level. **–Thibaut Munier, Numberly**

This is a mentality, it is not always a software. There is a term called Application Lifecycle Management or ALM, which is a critical piece to every deployment of CRM. It is understanding as an organization how you are going to handle enhancements, bug fixes, etc. over time. **–Alan Garcia, Microsoft**

Q: What are the differences between small business and large organizations with CRM? What does it take to set up a CRM stack? What are the distinctions between CRM and marketing automation?

The output is the same, although a large organization may have more people, more influencers, more decision-makers and more stakeholders. But ultimately you are coming up with the same output. In that sense, it doesn't matter whether it is an enterprise or a small business. It is important not just to think short-term about what you are trying to accomplish this quarter or this year, but also to think about a long-term path for where you want to go in the next two, three, four, five years. Things that you think you want to do five years from now may influence your design. **–Marc Kravitz, Microsoft**

It is a long process in enterprises and takes a lot of time to collaborate. In a smaller organization, you can move more quickly with what needs to be done and execute it faster. **– Nick Metcalfe, Saatachi & Saatachi**

I came into this company when their CRM had already been in place for a few years and everyone was doing their own thing. It was completely incoherent if you looked at it from a larger perspective. What one salesperson was doing might make sense to him or her, but if they were to leave, then no one would be able to make sense of what it was. Have clear rules and make sure that all of the terms are used the same throughout. **–Ronnie Kassiff, Inbound Marketing Consultant**

Q: What goes into setting up personas? How many personas make sense for what kinds of companies, and how do you use them?

One of the best ways to get accurate personas is by surveying your current clients that you want more of and not the clients that are difficult to work with. Survey these great clients and find out what success means to them, their demographics, the day-to-day issues in their current job and how you can help them as a company. From there, you will see patterns emerge, and you can narrow those down to a certain type of persona. The number of personas depends on the size of the company. You also want to see where they live, and if they live primarily on Facebook, then you want to focus more of your ad buys there. **–Ronnie Kassiff, Inbound Marketing Consultant**

Make sure that you are mining your data as a starting point and also make sure that you are talking to people. Talk to as many of your target customers as you can. They are surprisingly forthcoming when they know you are not there to sell them. **–Anita Taylor, Hopscotch**

Personas can also help your sales team. We had a persona at a company I worked with that we called "Owner Owen." He was a young owner of a company; you pick up the phone and call him but he hangs up. You send him an email; he unsubscribes. He is the type of person that doesn't like to be contacted very often unless it is something very high level, important, and quick. He will be off the phone in two minutes. That is something where it can help a salesperson to know that and say, "Okay this is an Owner Owen, so I need to not call him at a busy time and just send him an email that says, hey when you can chat? Here is my number." **–Ronnie Kassiff, Inbound Marketing Consultant**

Q: What CRM best practices do you suggest for businesses?

It is all about making sure that you can connect data (including behavioral data), decision science (what is that next logical ask?), and the communication (email, social, postcards). Too many companies focus on one of these aspects without combining all three. **–Nick Metcalfe, Saatachi & Saatachi**

You can never underestimate the power and proliferation of dirt, and by dirt, I mean that salespeople, in general, are notoriously not detail-oriented. You need to set up your CRM systems very clearly so that everyone follows the same process, it is easy to use and it's easy to keep things uniform. **–Anita Taylor, Hopscotch**

You can also create automated tasks on the backend, so if a salesperson puts in that this person was "busy" when they called, then you can automatically on the backend create a task that says "Call this person next week" as a reminder to the salesperson. **–Ronnie Kassiff, Inbound Marketing Consultant**

One of the values of a CRM platform is that you can transition the customer to be a service customer. Not every sales transaction leads to a customer that you would necessarily service, but if you are selling a product that needs service then you can transition those customers. In a CRM system, you can aggregate all of that data and from the 360 degree view you have a picture of what they have purchased, pitched, what products have been marketed to them, and you have the perspective of what they have to say about post-sale services, any problems they experienced, and how they are being treated after the purchase has gone through. **–Marc Kravitz, Microsoft**

Q: What are some tools that you have used to either manage a robust CRM program or pieces of a CRM program?

As someone from Microsoft, of course, I want to recommend Microsoft Dynamic CRM, but I will also recommend a few other things. I would recommend that you also look at DocumentDB–that is a data management tool that can help power and enhance your data methods. If you have your own custom applications, vendors can actually build and have applications running out of the marketplace for you. There are also third-party applications like Informatica, Zappier, and Microsoft Launch Flow. **–Alan Garcia, Microsoft**

We take this view that you need to have one central view of the customer across all of these different use cases or business units, so customer care needs to have the same view as marketing, advertising, commerce, and the research and analytics team. We are working towards one integrated platform.

Integration with other systems is really important. LiveRamp is doing a really cool thing to onboard data to different systems. Segment.io is making it easy to push data around. MParticle is doing it for mobile devices. At Sprinklr, putting all of those systems in one place and having all of those teams being able to collaborate in one place, getting unified reporting in one place, and governance for the enterprise so user permissioning is there as well. **–Erik Ober, Sprinklr**

Q: Where do you see, CRM going in the future? Where are we in the continuum of time relative to these tools and technologies?

I think that this is going to continue with blurring the lines between CRM and marketing automation systems. A lot of the systems coming out right now are an integrated version of the two rather than having a separate CRM system and a separate marketing automation system. For example, HubSpot and InfusionSoft are both two-in-one. **–Ronnie Kassiff, Inbound Marketing Consultant**

I think in the future a lot of it is going to be about making data actionable and being able to pull data out of all of your systems and bring it together. **–Anita Taylor, Hopscotch**

The future of CRM is going mobile and self-service. Organizations want to drive customers or potential customers to websites and be able to collect data there. **– Marc Kravitz, Microsoft**

From the customer standpoint, it is better relationships. But I see the dark side too. There is a creepy factor when I can see that you spent 1.2 minutes outside of my store. So, it's about figuring out a way to balance that. **–Nick Metcalfe, Saatachi & Saatachi**

Q: Are there any pitfalls to avoid, red flags, horror stories, worst practices?

The challenges are siloed. You can't really connect all of the dots that you need to connect. **–Nick Metcalfe, Saatachi & Saatachi**

I think the worst case is actually not high tech at all–it's low-tech and it's very common, which is that when you implement the system there is a big "hoorah" and there is training and it's all great. Then as the months and years go on, there is benign neglect. No one is really monitoring the system to see what is in there and no one cares what is in there until the day that you are trying to do some data analysis and you realize it is all garbage. Then it becomes a problem. After it has built up for 20 years and the data is useless, then it becomes a C-suite level problem. **–Anita Taylor, Hopscotch**

The most common issue that I see is people getting a CRM or marketing automation system as a knee-jerk reaction, saying, "Oh, my competitors have this. They are doing all of this stuff so we need this," but then they let it die or turn into garbage. You need to make sure that if you are going to invest, you have a clear plan and goals that you are building towards rather than buying this piece of software without understanding it or utilizing it. **–Ronnie Kassiff, Inbound Marketing Consultant**

Marketing Trends with IoT

Panelists help define the concept of the Internet of Things, how it collects actionable data about your customers; and what it means to the future of marketing.

Here are some key takeaways from this topic:

- **Mainstream use of IoT is still in the early stages**
  Whether your goal is to boost customer retention, streamline the manufacturing process, or monitoring your supply chain, we're still a long way off from realizing its full potential.
- **Companies have to strike a balance when it comes to privacy**
  Most customers are delighted to get real-time, value-added offers that are tailored to them based on their data–but if you go too far, the strategies you're using risk taking on a "Big Brother" vibe.
- **The benefits that come from IoT will be hidden to the customer but will improve customer experience exponentially**
  It might be soft marketing rather than overt, but if IoT helps services and products improve the customer experience, your company's reputation and sales will reflect that.

Q: IoT (Internet of Things) can be described in many different ways with many different definitions. What does it mean to you?

IoT is a device that is connected to the Internet in some way, but it does not give you Internet access. The FitBit is a good example. It is connected via your phone; there is a bridge technology. **–Dave Mathews, NewAer Proximity Platform**

The IoT concept arose because sensors are now able to directly communicate their data to the cloud or to servers. Before we used to think of a sensor as basically a very dedicated device where you could only read off data, and now it's become a smart device. You can reason about the data it's giving you in real time. Everybody's phone is pretty much both a computer and a sensor that can acknowledge where you are, which direction you're driving and so on. **– Swamy Narayanaswamy, Cs3 Inc.**

What are your favorite home/personal applications and your favorite applications from a corporate or professional standpoint?

Besides the Tesla, which is just beyond cool, I think my favorite current device is actually the Amazon Echo. I was in a test group for it way before it started shipping and I am completely in love with it. I am an applied physicist, my background is in wave theory, and I love audio. I think audio is going to be an incredibly powerful interface as we move forward. **–David Knight, Terbine**

My favorite thing in my professional life is essentially like a "situation room" in the supply chain field–kind of like Wolf Blitzer on election night. There is this big company that runs a supply chain management facility with touch screens all around and they have real time IoT data coming in, weather reports coming in, and if there's a storm in Singapore and their supplier there cannot get them their stuff, they have alternatives lined up to keep the supply chain moving. Very cool stuff. They have a 360-degree view where you can literally go up and touch the screen. **–Swamy Narayanaswamy, Cs3 Inc.**

Q: What are some other real-time, real-life examples where companies are using this data to make more intelligent business decisions?

It is really, really early. You are starting to see brands like Amazon with the Alexa platform and the Echo integrate it. For example, Alexa is an open platform, and the TV networks are using it for setting reminders as to when to tune into a show. But again, it's very, very early. **–Jay Symonds, Amazon**

Another example might be getting financing details sent to your phone for the car that you are standing in front of. With airlines, if you are walking through the airport and you have an hour before your flight, then maybe we will give you an offer for a restaurant–but if you have 10 minutes maybe it will be an offer for a coffee. This is sort of just-in-time information, but we are really early into the testing phases of these types of things. **–Dave Mathews, NewAer Proximity Platform**

Q: Is privacy still an issue, or have we gotten to the point where people just don't care anymore?

Depends on where you live. For example, in the United States, we are the opt-out society. The European community is opt-in. It depends on where you are on the platform right now. There is no such thing as a uniform body of law that handles these privacy issues on the planet right now. – **David Knight, Terbine**

I think privacy is always going to be an issue. We always have to weigh privacy vs. convenience, and the vendors are very good at getting you to the pain point. They know exactly when you're not reading the terms of an agreement. I have noticed that people in this country and culture are much more aware of when they are giving things up to the government–that brand is a negative brand right now–but with every other brand they are willing to give up data quite willingly. **–Swamy Narayanaswamy, Cs3 Inc.**

Did you know that almost all ATMs have a microphone in them and a lot of them have cameras? Those were put there so you could have a real-time interaction with a person, like a teller, and then they realized that you would be talking out loud when they said "What is your account number?" and everyone around you could hear, so it was a dumb idea, but someone else could place software there and use it for something else and that is interesting to me. **–David Knight, Terbine**

Years ago, Target was consuming data and purchasing data and they started targeting this household with pregnancy and new mom stuff. The dad of this household got so upset about the sheer volume of stuff that was coming in, he called Target and said, "Nobody in my house is pregnant– why are you sending me all of this stuff?" and they said, "Well, our data says that there is." The man said, "Well, it's not my wife." He went to talk to his daughter and his daughter was pregnant. So totally accurate but out of context about what was going on at the time. I think a lot of this is going to be in the experience and making sure that these marketing ads are not seen as intrusive or breaching someone's privacy. **–Jeff Marcoux, Microsoft**

Q: What are some of the methods and solutions to solve existing IoT problems?

We are working on a couple of things with airline companies right now that all tie back to customer experience. If we can do things like predictive maintenance on aircraft so that by the time the plane is landing you know what part needs to be replaced, the crew is ready, and both the parts and crew are on site, this helps you avoid keeping your customers stuck on an airplane or waiting for a flight. It is one of the most frustrating experiences as a customer, and it doesn't have to be that way. This is where a sensor can actually change the customer experience. **–Jeff Marcoux, Microsoft**

We haven't even scratched the surface of what IoT and AI will do for us. It is going to be a game-changer in many ways. Marketing is one where I think regulations and quality control will eventually have to be set up, but one example would include the agricultural industry. I was just talking to the California Head of Data Science for Agriculture, and the amount of impact that it will have on that field is amazing.

They are going to be able to monitor crops at a level that they could never have done before and provide the right amount of materials at the right times for the crops, which will change the game completely. **–Emad Hasan, Ex Facebook**

What about the moral ethics behind this technology for companies?

The reputation piece, the communicator's piece, and how you fit that backend are slowly going to become inseparable, because the only way that you solve for profiling is to run risk scenarios and decide where you are going to be transparent and communicate upfront that it is not perfect, but you are working on it. You also decide where you can't be transparent because of the "Big Brother" issue and how you work through that. Finally, you decide whether or not you need to test it to see if there are any hidden consequences and that will never be a perfect science. **–Robin Kim, Ruder Finn**

Q: What is the one unexpected lesson that you have learned as an IoT marketer?

Having seen a lot of these devices, it is astonishing how little the actual person at the end of the experience is accounted for. **–Sri Rao, Facebook**

The biggest learning is that I don't think it will be called IoT at some point. I think different technologies will come out of this and they will all be independent and I think it will be a completely different field by the time something is successful. **–Emad Hasan, Ex Facebook**

For me, I think it is the potential for how little changes can have a really big impact such as things like just in time delivery and starting to look at those components. The little things that allow brands to tweak the customer experience have a huge impact and often times they are things that you don't notice. **–Jeff Marcoux, Microsoft**

Predictive Analytics

Here are some key takeaways from this topic:

- **Know what you're looking for**
  The data can be overwhelming. Rather than trying to use all of it, hone in on the questions you really need answered and look for the patterns.
- **When you find a pattern, test it out**
  Predictive analytics are great at revealing trends. But if you change strategy based on that data, run another test to see if how your theory plays out in the new data.
- **Avoid the silo mentality**
  Merge, centralize and share data company-wide. Pull together teams from different areas to make it the data actionable.
- **Collect data even before you're ready to use it**
  There are so many tools for collecting data right now. If you wait until you have a clear idea of how to use the data, it won't be there when you need it.

Q: With so much data out there, what analytics are a good place to start?

The biggest thing that you have to do–especially on the brand side when you are trying to execute a campaign–is to figure out what your next step is. There is plenty of data available and lots of dashboards that will give you graphs, insights, and a conglomeration of things that you need a statistics degree to really understand.
What we have tried to do instead is to take all of those things and create next actions and probabilities around them. So if we know that there is a specific KPI that a brand is trying to maximize, we give the optimization portfolio for that particular KPI. We can look at their past campaigns, the types of influencers that have worked best with them, topicality, location, demographics, all of those things. It all becomes part of a predictive system that acts almost as a decision engine for those end users. **–Ben Williams, Reelio, Inc.**

If you know the rules and patterns that drive your business, a data expert can come into your business and help you a) capture that data and b) analyze it fast enough so that you can actually take advantage of it. **–Swamy Narayanaswamy, Cs3 Inc.**

When you think about data analysis and analytics in general, it is pattern matching. It is finding previous things that have happened and trying to build a pattern out of it. It can't tell you real predictions of the future, it can't predict unusual events. What it can do is give you a broad analysis and an idea of where you need to focus. It can help you find an area where something is happening that doesn't quite make sense, and then after you've taken the time to really dig into it, then you can use those tools to hone in on actual predictions and decision-making strategies. **–Ben Williams, Reelio, Inc.**

Think about it like this. Let's say you have 1,000 customers come through the door and 100 actually buy something. What makes those 100 interesting? So, you go back and look at their behavior and see what they did that is different from the 900 who didn't make a purchase. Then you can create a learning model, put in place a new rule and see if for the next 1,000 customers, does the prediction come true? **–Swamy Narayanaswamy, Cs3 Inc.**

Q: What tools are you using?

From the marketing perspective, we have varied email systems and automation systems we use including our internal product Dynamic Marketing (Microsoft), Marketo, and ExactTarget. We have a great social platform that we are pulling all kinds of data from called Sprinklr, and then we consolidate all of that data into another platform. Then we overlaid a ton of machine-learning algorithms over that so we can start to build out the models around that. **–Jeff Marcoux, Microsoft**

We use a lot of tools that startups use. On the descriptive and analytic side, we use Tableau. On the modeling side, we use SAS data modeling. We have a few data scientists on board as well who work on predictive models. **–Mihir Korke, The Lending Club**

Kissmetrics is a great tool for individual data. If you can tie the individual data information back to your data set and work to build your target markets, then that is very powerful. **–Dave Rogers, ConvertClick Digital Analytics**

An IBM product that we use is called AlchemyAPI. It is a very cheap, inexpensive, API that allows you to put in text data and it gives you a one–or two-word summary of that data, and then you can structure it. So, you can feed AlchemyAPI 1,000 tweets and it will say, 300 of these tweets are about technology, 100 are about fashion. It also does things like share what language those tweets are written in. **–Jesse Leimgruber, NeoReach**

IBM has quite a few options, which are all organized under Watson. You can input all this data including social media data and you can set API, which can help you to identify patterns and help you to merge this data with your existing data. **–Dr. Alex Liu, IBM**

There are some really simple tools out there like Google Trends. Trend data is something that is a bit more accurate than actual predictions. With Google Trends, you type in any keyword and Google will say, "We have seen that every May this keyword goes up," so you can make better sense of trends. **–Jesse Leimgruber, NeoReach**

Q: What challenges do you see with data from a marketing perspective?

There isn't a common data structure or common way to merge all of the data together. One of the biggest pitfalls that we came across early on was that we had a lot of tools, and we needed to get that insight across the entire company. Instead, we had a lot of different groups not talking to each other.

Now we are trying to combine that data and centralize it through our internal data management platform called Cosmos. Our strategy is to suck in all of that data, normalize it and then do actionable intelligence on top of that. It comes down to tools, normalizing the data, and then how you make that actionable. **–Jeff Marcoux, Microsoft**

You need to understand the data and make sure that you don't let the tools make the final decision. This is huge. I worked with a giant e-commerce site a couple of years back, with millions of dollars in sales, and they looked at Google Analytics to see which marketing channel got them the most revenue. Google Analytics attributes a sale based on which marketing channel sent the last visitor. So, if a visitor Googled the company and then clicked on an ad of the company and then clicked on a Facebook ad of the company and made a purchase, Facebook gets all of the credit for the sale even though there were multiple other channels involved in the process. So, they said, "We have to double down on Adwords." Meanwhile, their press was driving all of the awareness. So, the tools can be very misleading. **–Jesse Leimgruber, NeoReach**

What are some of the key skill sets you need to work in predictive marketing and analytics? When hiring new workers, what do you look for?

For me, having the stats background is important, but the other piece that I look for is a social science background in sociology, psychology, something that shows that you are interested in the world. I want to know that you are curious and that you have a natural inclination to figure things out, to peel back the layers. **–Dave Rogers, ConvertClick Digital Analytics**

I look for three skills. Firstly, SQL. Then R or Python. It doesn't matter which, because if you know one you can learn the other quickly. Third, how to visualize the data.
I think that is the biggest challenge. If I have a data scientist on my team who writes the best code but can't present it, then that is a problem. **–Mayank Johri, First Republic Bank**

Q: Share an example of when you used predictive analytics for marketing.

When I was at PayPal, one of the things we were looking at was customer segmentation. We would bring in a marketing agency who would say, "These are their archetypes as customers," but one approach that we did a bit differently involved machine learning to figure out customer segments. We found a cluster that was buying a lot of women's products, men's products, electronics, motorcycles, and we could not figure out what was going on. Eventually, we figured out that these guys were essentially couples that were using the same login ID to log in to their PayPal account. **–Emad Hassan, Ex Facebook**

What advice would you give to businesses to get ahead of the game in predictive analytics in the next two years?

First of all, are you looking at all of the data that you can gather from various sources? Are you looking at the people who are visiting your website and collecting all of the information on them beyond the IP address? My advice would be to harness everything that you can and to not leave anything on the table for the moment. If you miss something, there is a competitor out who that hasn't missed it and is now ahead of you. **–Mihir Korke, The Lending Club**

Number one, start learning data and connect teams. Do things, get together and start pushing things around. You might have to prove the case at some point, you might not. Number two, if you are going to compete with predictive analytics specifically for marketing then raise your hand and put some money on the table. Take it seriously. Put some effort and energy behind making sure that the data is solid, everyone trusts it, and the connecting points are working. Get some real people doing the work and don't make it a back-burner project. Number three, put teams together. The most successful teams I've seen are made up of predictive analytics folks and data science folks talking to BI. BI has the data, the structure, and the warehouse. BI is your friend, so put them in the same room together. I often don't see that in the beginning, and that is a problem. **–Dave Rogers, ConvertClick Digital Analytics**

Tracking Post-Click Activity with BI Tools

Here are some key takeaways from this topic:

- **Conversion is the ultimate goal, but it starts with building a relationship with the customer**
  If someone doesn't bite on their first visit to the site, you can still take steps to keep them interested and thinking about your brand. Don't neglect the long term.
- **Know your demographic for each post**
  Go to Google Analytics and see what the demographic is for each post, so you know what you need to write if you need to write a certain way, and where you need to post it.
- **Collect every touch point**
  By using only the first source where the customer came into your campaign or the last click and assuming that that counts for all of the different touch points, you can't draw accurate conclusions. You need a more holistic view.
- **Embrace BI technologies**
  You shouldn't only select one predictive analytics platform. Use a blend of platforms that makes the most sense for your application.

Q: What does post-click activity mean to you, and how do you best optimize it? What is your perspective on the journey consumers take?

From the blogger side, I use Google Analytics and see what the demographic is for each post so I know what I need to write, if I need to write a certain way, and where I need to post it. Looking at how long people are staying on the page is another thing that I look at. **–Shereen Lavi, Rayan Enterprises**

I am primarily concerned with understanding which key metrics are significantly correlated with sales so that we are delivering our campaigns to drive revenue through sales. **– Vanessa Shanahan, Wunderman**

You need to figure out how to influence your audience while keeping a good rapport with them. You want to influence your audience to take the actions that serve your business goals, drive the bottom line and things like that, but you don't want to be pushy.
We are really looking at omni channel now, whether you are entering the customer journey on your phone or through a social media platform or even through IoT. There are a lot of data points to collect and dive into that you need to visualize and make sense of in order to be successful. **– Jacob Warwick, ThinkWarwick Communications**

It is not just about getting data or converting something. It is more about, what is that desirable action? When you visit an Apple store it is less about the transaction and more about creating that relationship the moment you walk through the door. Your website has to act in the same way

---

with a strong call to action and a simple call to action. –
Ramkumar Ravichandran, Visa

There is a lot of competition in driving folks to our websites. One thing you can do is build a lot of content. Backlinks drive people to your site, and that is where you want them to go. A few years ago, it was "Send them to a social media platform," but people do not backlink from those social media pages.

If you put something on your website, people have to share that link and get their friends to your site where you can guide them through and take them on the customer journey. As you guide them to recommended articles and other things, you are grabbing more post-click data as well. We know 78% of consumers do not want to talk to sales. They want to gather their own information. You want your website to be that resource. **–Eric Mitchell, Penguin Strategies**

Q: What are your opinions and insights on last touch and multi-touch?

You have to look holistically at the customer experience. What is the customer's journey? Where is, the brand touching the customer? The first part is really understanding, "Do we have a full holistic view of the brand's impact on the consumer?" And many times, the answer to this question is no. Sometimes a consumer is touched five, 10, maybe even 15 times before they ultimately convert. By using only, the first source where they came into your campaign or the very last click and assuming that that counts for all of the different touchpoints, you

cannot draw any conclusions. You are missing needed data.
–Vanessa Shanahan, Wunderman

Q: What are some tools you use as input on helping to make decisions on increasing engagement or ensuring that your web users are performing some desirable action, such as Hubspot, Google Analytics, and Adobe SiteCatalyst?

I have done most of my research and predictive analytics work on Hana and it is an extremely powerful database. The NBA runs all of their analytics on it. Another one would be DataSift, and they enhance the data. They are the database, they take the data and then they enhance it and make inferences for you. **–Shereen Lavi, Rayan Enterprises**

The big data collectors, Microsoft and Oracle and others, have all acquired predictive analytic platforms in the space and I think if you can marry that data usually makes the most sense. Adobe has Business Catalyst and Facebook has Facebook Insights. You shouldn't only select one but really use a blend of platforms that makes the most sense for your application. **–Sinan Kanatsiz, Chapman5**

From a platform perspective, I love all the API plug-and-play platforms. I think for non-Amazon and large companies, that makes sense because it's cost-efficient, pre-built, and solves 99% of our problems. Clarabridge is a great unstructured data analysis platform where you can pull in all of your unstructured data and analyze it alongside your social. Affinio is another cool tool to be able to understand your followers in terms of segments and tribes, and how you might have very distinct subsets within your overall followers. **–Vanessa Shanahan, Wunderman**

Tableau has been really great, very actionable stuff that marketers can use. Mixpanel is another great tool. For the social marketers, out there, Simply Measured is a really good easy to understand tool. The biggest thing to keep in mind when using these tools is not to dive too deep too soon. Start with your general business questions and make sure you are tracking those correctly as well as answering them. Then you can scale your data and start diving deeper. **– Jacob Warwick, ThinkWarwick Communications**

As a marketer, I don't want to just know what is happening but also where I could be, and that is where the Adobe suite comes into play. You can know where customers are coming from as well as their likes and dislikes. This makes it possible to target them and retarget them. Another tool is Google 360. **–Ramkumar Ravichandran, Visa**

I like a tool called TrendKit right now, new on the scene with the ability to attribute upper funnel activities to the web. It's a great dashboard and I'm trying to use it and integrate it with everything else that I'm using. Quid is really great, powerful tool. Marketshare is great for mixed media modeling. Unmetric is another one where you can look at content that is highly compelling and if your teams are tasked with building content, it is an opportunity to be able to keyword query other highly compelling content and see what is out there that other consumers are highly engaged with. **–Vanessa Shanahan, Wunderman**

Kissmetrics is a great tool for post-click analytics. Sprout Social is a favorite of mine for social analytics. **–Eric Mitchell, Penguin Strategies**

IBM Watson has started adding a variety of new applications that they want to bring to everyday people and not just businesses. They are even doing it for sports. **–Shereen Lavi, Rayan Enterprises**

Q: When you are counseling clients, how often are you looking at analytics such as abandon rate? And how quickly are you able to shift the way you build a call to action or change the messaging?

What do you really want to achieve? You must first have the goal and then make sure that your technology setup reflects that goal or goals. If you want to make a change, you look at your testing process, and it could mean practically making changes every half hour for a large company or every few days as a small company. **–Karthikeyan Kandasamy, Visa**

Don't overreact. I have seen this a lot when measuring campaign performance with clients. Clients will automatically go to what performed best last click, last touch. They will start wiping video out of the plan, start wiping high-end ad placements out of the plan. Anything that is upper funnel just goes straight out, and the overall campaign effectiveness in the months after declines. **–Jay Symonds, Amazon**

Oftentimes you get so excited about the marketing and the promotion, and you are driving things on social, but you are not properly tracking things. So, you don't know where your dollars are going or where your influence is coming from. Implementation is key even if it is just basic Google Analytics. You have to be tagging things with UTM parameters, and you have to really understand where your influence is going so that as you start to scale you can say, "Okay, now Facebook is an actual platform, because we are getting 20% of our revenue from it." You can actually follow the journey back to your website. **–Jacob Warwick, ThinkWarwick Communications**

Q: Where is, the future going? Where should we be going with this?

There are a couple of companies that I recommend you check out in regard to where post-click activity is headed in the future. One is Radius.com, a business intelligence application that is connected into Salesforce and other CRMs to better understand how marketing and the customer journey play a part in getting customers into the CRM. Another company is Curalate. They study images and the way that they are shared and how that converts to commerce. Another one I recommend is TokyWoky. They allow customers on websites who have questions to ask all of the other visitors on the website and they identify those individuals that respond back as an ambassador. The whole activity and web experience is now shifting into these unique micro apps. **–Sinan Kanatsiz, Chapman5**

Security and Privacy in the Cloud

Digital security is a major hot-button issue for every company, organization, individual or even government body. We added a special session to our conference to discuss the best ways you can help secure your company's and customer's data, whether on-site or on the cloud.

Here are some key takeaways from this topic:

- **There is no right or wrong answer when it comes to storing data on the cloud vs. on premise**
  You need to assess how secure your own system is compared to the cloud vendor you're considering and make the determination that way.
- **No one is immune to security breaches, but you can take steps to minimize risk**
  These include everything from making sure third-party providers who access your data have adequate security protection to using common sense about opening emails from unknown parties.
- **Use multi-factor authentication**
  Requiring additional components for a user to gain access is always more secure.

Q: First of all, how would you define the "cloud"? Cloud is a term like IoT that gets thrown out often, but what does it mean?

There is the technical definition of cloud: broad network access, ubiquitous, etc. In essence, it is typically third-party owned if it is going to be considered a public cloud such as Amazon and AT&T. With broad network access, anyone can access it typically, and by "ubiquitous" I mean it is easy to use and metered with a subscription fee, something that would be considered an operational expense. The goal is placing data or a business process or service out on the Internet where you can scale and increase or decrease your usage as necessary. **–Ariston Collander, AT&T**

When you take your data and off of your server and put it onto somebody else's server, that is the cloud. **–Kevin Haley, Symantec**

"Cloud" is very vast, so I will throw a couple of things out to frame the conversation. First, I would throw out that you can look at the National Institute of Science and Technology where they have a very good diagram that gives you the various components of cloud technologies. I do agree that most of the conversation occurs around public cloud, but private cloud is also critical. **–Peter Lopez, Technicolor**

Q: What are your thoughts on cloud vs. on premise? What is more secure?

It comes down to who can secure your data best. If an entity is mature and confident that they are going to have better security than whatever cloud vendor they are considering, then that's great and they shouldn't put that data in the cloud. Conversely, if the cloud vendor is able to secure it better and bring more resources to it than you are, then, by all means, put your data with the cloud vendor that is going to keep your data more secure. Companies are of all different sizes, maturities, and resource levels so look at where your company is in regards to security. **–Michael Machado, RingCentral, Inc.**

You also have to realize that your computers are not secure by design. You have to secure them. Many of the breaches that we see happen because someone finds a bug in the operating system and the vendors fix that, but the customer has not updated and the server is still vulnerable. You need to ensure that your software is always up to date. **–Ambuj Kumar, Rambus**

The Cloud Security Alliance publishes a list of due diligence questions that you should be asking any cloud vendor. It is also important to realize that it's not just the data in the cloud that is at risk. Endpoints and social engineering are often the targets or at the very least the beginning of the chain that leads to a data breach. **–Michael Machado, RingCentral, Inc.**

Q: What about API (application programming interfaces)? Talk about API and tapping into these clouds, and what you need to know about best practices.

In the late 80s, APIs became a way for people to really share information and leverage an entryway into a vast network of applications that can all work together. Previously, there was not a standardized format for apps to communicate with one another, but over the last 20 or 30 years, we have gotten to the point where machines are talking to machines and actually making decisions without human interaction at all. That is where we get to business intelligence and automation among other things. **–Peter Lopez, Technicolor**

Q: What are the questions that we should be asking the tool vendors available today such as Google Drive before integrating these tools with our own technology and data?

Read the privacy policy and understand that. If you are not equipped to be able to do that then make sure you bring in a trusted party to help you. You need to know how your information is going to be treated, which is going to dictate whether that is the right solution for you or not. **–Ray Espinoza, Proofpoint**

All of these communications should be encrypted, the data at rest and the data in motion. Meanwhile, you need to assess your own security by asking, "What is talking to what, by what means, how often, and with what frequency?" You have to understand the data and the legality around the data to perform your own risk assessment. Database access monitoring and web application firewall technology can help address these parts of the problem. **–Ryan Potter, Rambus**

Q: What does it mean when content is locked on your laptop, but the key to the locked content is stored in the cloud?

One of the challenges that you are going to face is getting access to your data. When it is encrypted, if you lose that key, that data is gone. There is no way to get that information back. So, what is the secondary method for me to back up that key so that I can retrieve that information if I can't get access to the device? The problem is that as soon as you start storing keys in the cloud in a system over which you have no control, you are placing trust in that cloud storage or wherever that key is going and whoever has access to that key. At the company level, it comes down to trusting these third parties and having a program in place where you are validating that wherever this key is going is trustworthy. You have to trust they have the right security mechanisms in place to keep that information safe. **–Ariston Collander, AT&T**

Fundamentally, everybody needs to start looking at compartmentalized exposure. You need to start to classify your devices and your data, separating the passwords and keys so that there is not just one key that unlocks everything. **–Peter Lopez, Technicolor**

The weakest link in a chain isn't necessarily the device in your hand. It could be the network that those run across as well. Creating an encryption standard that is outside of what the companies give you is a necessary best practice. **–Dave Mathews, NewAer Proximity Platform**

Q: How do breaches occur, and what do you do if it happens?

Phishing is one of the most popular methods. Sometimes you get an email or pop-up that might look like spam or it

---

might look like something that you should open up. We like to think that we don't fall for this, but the data shows that we do. We click on things and open things that lead to malware on our endpoints. You have to think about not only how encrypted or secure your own data is but also who has access to your data, because if they're targeted, that puts you at risk too. **–Michael Machado, RingCentral, Inc.**

Your company is only as good as its weakest link. If you bring in third-party providers to plug into your network to provide an added-value service, and their security controls are not at the same levels as your security, then you have to treat that area as untrusted. **–Ray Espinoza, Proofpoint**

Breaches can also occur due to passwords that aren't secure enough. A good answer is to use a password manager. They are very affordable, most have enforcement capabilities, and they have everything from the small, sole-proprietorship level to the enterprise solution that incorporates two-factor authentication. **–Ryan Potter, Rambus**

Q: What are some of the best practices and ideas of companies or products that everyone here can take away from this and use?

The obvious one is two-factor authentication. The cloud can have all of the security in the world, but if the end user's login and password are phished, then the attacker has access to all of their information. Two-factor authentication involves having two things to allow for a login such as a password and a pin. **–Kevin Haley, Symantec**

At the enterprise level, understand who in your company is doing what in terms of sending data out to third parties. You may not want someone in the finance department finding a business out there who could provide business analytics and suddenly they are sending a whole bunch of financial information out. DLP–data loss prevention software–can be run locally or on the server and tries to do some matching to look for credit card information, etc. and keep it from being sent out. A cloud access security broker is another option where a stream of data is sent to a security service, which is typically cloud-based, and they look at your traffic and monitor it to figure out what information is being transferred. **–Ariston Collander, AT&T**

Multifactor authentication is becoming the new standard and includes three or more factor authentications to get into any account. **–Peter Lopez, Technicolor**

Forty-six percent of all targeted attacks are directed at companies with fewer than 250 employees. Two lessons to take away from that: 1) You can go into the smaller company to get to the bigger company, and 2) Small companies have information that is worth stealing. **–Kevin Haley, Symantec**

Q: What does security look like in three years?

At work, we are all exposed to "Bring your own device." It sounds great for companies. They don't have to buy you a laptop or buy you a phone because you are going to bring your device. Well, by bringing your device you just brought anything and everything that you connected to previously

---

into your business. You then have to think about, is this device hostile or not? **–Peter Lopez, Technicolor**

The next thing will be agents. There is a lot of bot talk these days, and then there are the voice interface platforms such as Amazon Echo or Siri. Voice interface is going to be interesting because of the amount of processing power it takes to understand my voice and its subtle nuances compared to yours. It is nearly impossible to do in a device right now. **–Dave Mathews, NewAer Proximity Platform**

The only thing that you can trust is a physical separation. **– Peter Lopez, Technicolor**

Appendix

Tools

Contributors

Businesses

Thank you to the following people that helped to make this book possible:

Elisa Croft: Your content marketing skills, event production skills and website skills are incredible. I am so fortunate to have you on our team and I adore your positive attitude. This project (and several others) could not have been possible without you.

Aoife Teague: Thank you for helping us to coordinate our 2017 conferences and for proofing much of our content.

Linda-Marie Koerner: Thank you for editing the videos that made this content. Without your hustle, this would not have been possible.

Thank you for reading the Medialeaders.com Digital Marketing Tactics book!

If you enjoyed some of these tips, please tweet your favorite quotes and include @MediaLeaders on Twitter so we can retweet you.

Also be sure to join our newsletter to be the first to hear about our next events MediaLeaders.com

Thanks,
@JoshOchs

P.S. Get exclusive access to our video collection by visiting MediaLeaders.com/dmt/videos

Notes

Consider mentioning @MediaLeaders on social

Notes

Notes

Consider mentioning @MediaLeaders on social

Notes

Notes

Consider mentioning @MediaLeaders on social

Notes

Notes

Consider mentioning @MediaLeaders on social

Notes

Notes

Consider mentioning @MediaLeaders on social

Notes

_____

_____

_____

_____

_____

_____

_____

_____

_____

_____

_____

_____

_____

_____

_____

_____

Notes

Consider mentioning @MediaLeaders on social

Notes

Notes

Consider mentioning @MediaLeaders on social

Notes

Notes

Consider mentioning @MediaLeaders on social

Notes

Notes

Consider mentioning @MediaLeaders on social

Notes

Notes

_____

_____

_____

_____

_____

_____

_____

_____

_____

_____

_____

_____

_____

_____

_____

Consider mentioning @MediaLeaders on social

Notes

Notes

Consider mentioning @MediaLeaders on social

Notes

Notes

Consider mentioning @MediaLeaders on social

Notes

Notes

Consider mentioning @MediaLeaders on social

Notes

Notes

Consider mentioning @MediaLeaders on social

Notes

Made in the USA
Middletown, DE
29 July 2017